Weird, Wacky and Wild

ARIZONA TRIVIA

Paul Soderberg & Lisa Wojna
Illustrations by Peter Tyler, Roger
Garcia & Patrick Hénaff

BLUE
BIKE
BOOKS

The Publisher: Blue Bike Books
Website: www.bluebikebooks.com

Library and Archives Canada Cataloguing in Publication

Soderberg, Paul   Arizona trivia : weird, wacky & wild / Paul Soderberg
& Lisa Wojna.

ISBN 13: 978-1-897278-49-9
ISBN 10: 1-897278-49-7

　　1. Arizona--Miscellanea. I. Wojna, Lisa, 1962- II. Title.

F811.S65 2008   979.1   C2008-903897-5

Project Director: Nicholle Carrière
Project Editor: Kathy van Denderen
Production: Alexander Luthor
Cover Image: Courtesy of JupiterImages Corporation
Illustrations: Peter Tyler, Roger Garcia, Patrick Hénaff

We acknowledge the support of the Alberta Foundation for the Arts for our publishing program.

Alberta
Foundation
for the Arts

PC: 05

DEDICATION

For Geoff.

—PS

To my new friend from the Grand Canyon State—it's been a blast!

—LW

CONTENTS

ACKNOWLEDGMENTS

Grand Canyon–size thanks to the weird, wacky, wild and wonderful writing team of Lisa Wojna and Kathy van Denderen, to my friend Faye Boer, and to my mother, Betty Lee, who taught me to love books and would have loved this one.

–PS

Writing is typically a solitary occupation, but with a great co-author like Paul, it seemed so much less so. Thank you. I'll think about the rattlesnakes.

As always, thank you to Kathy van Denderen, whose patience as an editor and keen eye for detail is beyond compare. To my friend and mentor Faye, and to my publisher, Nicholle, who allows me to get to know my southern neighbors through these trivia projects—my list of travel destinations is increasing by the day.

And every day I thank God for the support I receive through family and friends. Without these dear people in my life, this and anything else I do would be meaningless.

–LW

INTRODUCTION

Ever since the Navajo and the Apache migrated from Canada down into Arizona around 1300 AD, this state has been a magnet for dreams of a better life. In the succeeding 700 years, people have continued to come here from all over the world in search of freedom, health, wealth and happiness.

As this book details, the first non-Native person ever to see the Grand Canyon was a Moor from North Africa. Arizona's greatest gold mine was discovered by a German. Tucson became a city because of an Italian; Phoenix was founded by a man from South Carolina, Flagstaff by a man from Washington, DC, and Scottsdale by a New Yorker. The cumulative effect of those people and countless others coming here in search of a better life has been to make Arizona a great place to live.

Of course, in Arizona, just like anywhere else, the old has not always reacted favorably to the arrival of the new. This book details the skeletons in Arizona's closet—the time when Native Americans were slaughtered for the bounty on their scalps, the night when machine guns mounted on armored personnel carriers shot rounds into Phoenix homes, the years of internment of Japanese Americans, the decade across which raged the deadliest blood feud in American history between a family of cattlemen and a family of sheepherders, and on and on. But the truth is that for every shameful incident, there have been thousands of triumphs, successes and positive developments, as this book also proudly details.

You hardly need a guidebook to appreciate this state. The first view of the Grand Canyon, the first sight of the world's most gigantic cactus soaring 50 feet high and weighing 12 tons, catching a world-class northern pike or trout or channel catfish in an Arizona river or lake—the sense of awe, amazement and delight sparked by such things requires no prior knowledge of Arizona.

But knowledge does deepen appreciation. The best example is the land itself. From central to southern Arizona, the land *looks* barren, just a hot desert. But that land literally teems with life, including 334 species of butterfly and 3900 species of plants.

Arizona's most "Old West" plant isn't Arizonan, by the way, but Ukrainian. It's the Russian thistle, brought over by early settlers, a round, bushy plant that grows three feet high, dies, cracks off and then goes rolling off across the desert as…a tumbleweed. Each dead Russian thistle tumbles with a purpose, to scatter its 250,000 seeds.

Knowing trivia like that leads to an appreciation of this state that is hardly trivial. The purpose of this book full of weird, wacky and wild trivia is, in a fun way, to truly deepen and enrich the enjoyment of anyone and everyone, first-time visitor or long-time resident, for this amazing state. From Arizona's geography to its environment and weather to its people and communities to its history, economy, politics, science and technology, law and crime, education, sports, it is all to be found in these pages.

You can certainly watch a game of basketball and enjoy it. But your appreciation of the game is deepened by this nugget of trivia: basketball was invented by a Canadian, and James Naismith's game was only the modern form of the game that for many centuries was the most popular sport among Arizona's prehistoric Indians. You can go happily about your business in Phoenix and know little or nothing about the city—but it's more fun to know that the city used to be called Pumpkinville, that one of its leaders believed himself to be a reincarnated Egyptian pharaoh and that employees and guests at one of Phoenix's best-loved hotels keep reporting sightings of the ghost of a schoolgirl who wanders the hallways crying.

Sometimes trivia is less entertaining than educational, and these kinds of facts are also to be found in these pages. For example, it's useful—even life-saving—to know that during Arizona's monsoon season, the Mogollon Rim ("moe-ge-own"), the 2000-foot escarpment where the low desert gives way to the high mountains, becomes very dangerous as the second-most lightning-struck place on the planet.

Other times, trivia plays the important role of puncturing urban legends, of unmasking "truths." For example, plenty of Arizonans will tell you earnestly and proudly that Arizona has the nation's highest per capita boat ownership—which is only true if you count toy boats for the bathtub, because of the 50 states, we rank 31st. It's common knowledge that in Arizona, it is unlawful to have more than one dildo in a house or to let a donkey sleep in your bathtub—but both are untrue: there are no such state laws. (On the other hand, it is indeed unlawful here to tease a Gila monster, and it used to be illegal, but no longer is, to hunt camels in Arizona.)

Fun or useful or eye-opening, the trivia in this book is guaranteed to deepen and enrich your appreciation of this truly incredible state, which is both very, very old, and startlingly new. There are still residents who remember the days before statehood in 1912 and still plenty of people whose lives overlapped the life of Wyatt Earp, who died in 1929.

Arizona is one of America's leading high-tech states, and we have the largest nuclear power plant in the nation. But it was also the home of people who built the largest and most sophisticated irrigation system in the ancient world, 1000 years ago. Scottsdale wasn't incorporated until 1951—and up the road a few hundred miles is Oraibi, the oldest continuously inhabited community in the United States, founded nine centuries ago.

So, welcome to a wealth of weird, wacky and wild trivia about this truly remarkable place. Columnist George Will once observed, "Baseball, it is said, is only a game. True. And the Grand Canyon is only a hole in Arizona. Not all holes, or games, are created equal." A single visit to the Grand Canyon State, either in person or through this book, is all you need to realize that not all American states are created equal.

AMAZING ARIZONA

It Began With Beavers

Some 90,000 people move to Arizona each year (that's 1730 new residents per week) and 31.7 million visit (86,849 tourists per *day*), and most of them say, "Wow!" even though there aren't that many beavers left.

The European settlement of both Canada and Arizona began with the fur trade and trappers who in effect said, "Wow, look at all the beavers!" According to one of Canada's greatest writers, Margaret Atwood, "Canada was built on dead beavers." And the first two Americans to set foot on Arizona soil were

Sylvester Pattie and his son James, who spent the winter of 1825 trapping beaver just south of where Phoenix would be founded a half century later. But in both Canada and Arizona, the initial "Wow!" for fur was immediately followed by expressions of amazement for everything else about the "new" land—especially the great diversity of the land itself.

An Amazing Place

Much of Arizona is flat; but Mount Whitney in California is the highest mountain in the Lower 48 states only because Arizona's highest mountain blew off the top 4000 feet. The state sits on the northern end of the largest, hottest and most barren terrain on the continent, the Great Sonoran Desert—but it also has a tiny jungle, a perpetual ice-cave and an area where low temperatures and short growing seasons hinder the growth of trees: a tundra.

Amazing Diversity

As with the land, so it is with almost everything else about the state, including its people. In fact, there is greater cultural diversity in Arizona than virtually anywhere else. Students of more than 140 nationalities attend Arizona State University, which is the largest university in the United States. And what about Cesar Chavez, who founded the United Farm Workers and whose birthday is celebrated in eight states? He was born in Arizona, the state that also has 21 different Native American tribal councils and nations. One of them, the Navajo Nation, is bigger than Massachusetts, Connecticut, Rhode Island and New Jersey combined.

Arizona (and this book) is full of things that might well make you say, "Wow!" But there are a few things that this amazingly diverse state *doesn't* have: hurricanes, California-style mudslides, dangerous earthquakes or major floods. Very few mosquitoes. And no supertanker oil spills.

JUST THE FACTS

What's in a Name?

There's a lot of history behind the naming of Arizona—and a whole lot of disagreement as well. Some suggest there's a little bit of Spanish influence in the name, stemming from a 1736 Spanish miner who put down stakes in the area after discovering silver. He named the area *Real de Arissona*. There are, however, several other suggestions as to the origin of Arizona. One theory posits it quite possibly stems from a number of Native American words: *arizuma* from the Aztecs or *arizonac* from the Pima. In the first instance the Indian term refers to "silver-bearing" and in the second, it refers to "little spring place." Another theory is that the word is a version of the Papago Indian word *ali-shonak* (small spring) or *aleh-zon* (young spring).

DID YOU KNOW?

The first time the name "Arizona" officially appeared was on a map made by Father Ignaz Pfeffercorn, a German Jesuit living in Sonora, in 1794.

Also Known As

We'd place money on it that anyone venturing into Arizona to visit the Grand Canyon wouldn't be surprised to know the state's best-known nickname is "Grand Canyon State." A lesser known but equally worthy moniker is "Copper State," named after the area's wealth of minerals. When the Arizona Territory was formed in 1863, its given name wasn't a shoe-in. Other possible names for the new territory included "Gadsonia," "Pimeria," "Montezuma" and "Arizuma." But the prize for "Worst Name Idea" goes to Father Eusebio Kino, who, in 1704, recommended that southern Arizona, the land of the Pima, be called "New Philippines." This was after the Spaniards had already misnamed the Indians themselves—their word for "No!" was *"Pim!"* so the Spaniards called them Pimas.

Making It Official
The first European explorer known to have landed in Arizona was a French Franciscan named Marcos de Niza back in 1539—which was 81 years before the Pilgrims aboard the *Mayflower* landed at Plymouth Rock. After de Niza, others came to the area seeking out a new land to conquer and colonize, and for a time it was under first Spanish and then Mexican reign, as detailed in the History section of this book.

If You're From Here

Folks living in Arizona are called Arizonans. Prescott is pronounced, "PRESS-cut," Tempe is "Tem-PEE," and of course, Tucson is "TOO-sawn."

DID YOU KNOW?

Arizona's state motto is *Ditat Deus,* Latin for "God Enriches."

OFFICIALLY ARIZONA

Statehood with a Bang

At the announcement on February 14, 1912, that Arizona was officially a state, people everywhere fired their pistols into the air, miners in Bisbee set off dynamite, citizens in Snowflake set off a gigantic explosion, and a 48-gun salute was begun in Phoenix—and halted after 38 shots because the booming was rattling windows and panicking horses.

The Great Seal

Adopted in 1912, the Great Seal of the State of Arizona is centered by a crest that shows off the mountainous countryside, the warmth of the sun, and a miner with pickaxe and shovel—a salute to the state's mining industry. The crest is surrounded by the words "Great Seal of the State of Arizona 1912."

INANIMATE STATE SYMBOLS

Flying High

If asked to describe the Arizona State Flag, we'd have to say it looks like a ray of sunshine. Thirteen rays of red and gold, centered by a star, fill the top half of the flag, perched on top of a sea of blue covering the bottom half. But the choices of color and symbols are more than just a stunning creation. The 13 rays represent the country's 13 founding colonies, as well as the setting sun. The colors, while representative of the sun, are also significant in that they were the colors carried in 1540 by Spaniards looking for the "Seven Cities of Cibol." The blue represents the "Liberty blue" of the national flag, and the copper-colored star represents Arizona's copper industry. The flag as we know it today was designed by Colonel Charles W. Harris in 1912. He based the design on an earlier flag he had created for the Arizona Rifle Team in 1910. It was officially adopted as the state flag on February 17, 1917.

Singing Loud and Proud!

Arizona joins 48 of its sister states in having an official state song. In fact, there are two. The first "anthem" was originally called "Arizona" and later renamed the "Arizona March Song." Written in 1915 by Margaret Rowe Clifford, with music by Maurice Blumenthal, the song speaks of a land with broad valleys and winding rivers, a land rich in gold and silver and awash in sunshine—no wonder it's such a magnet for tourists and snowbirds! That song was first published by the Hatch Music Company of Philadelphia, adopted as the state song on February 28, 1919, and is in the public domain:

Come to this land of sunshine
To this land where life is young.
Where the wide, wide world is waiting,
The songs that will now be sung.
Where the golden sun is flaming
Into warm, white, shining day,
And the sons of men are blazing
Their priceless right of way.
Come stand beside the rivers
Within our valleys broad.
Stand here with heads uncovered,
In the presence of our God!
While all around, about us
The brave, unconquered band,
As guardians and landmarks
The giant mountains stand.
Not alone for gold and silver
Is Arizona great.
But with graves of heroes sleeping,
All the land is consecrate!
O, come and live beside us

However far ye roam
Come and help us build up temples
And name those temples "home."
CHORUS:
Sing the song that's in your hearts
Sing of the great Southwest,
Thank God, for Arizona
In splendid sunshine dressed.
For thy beauty and thy grandeur,
For thy regal robes so sheen
We hail thee Arizona
Our Goddess and our queen.

In 1982, an official alternate anthem was chosen. Entitled simply "Arizona", written by Rex Allen Jr., this version highlights several mountain ranges—the Dos Cabezas (or "two peaks") Mountains Wilderness and the Superstition Mountains—and hints at the state's colorful history with "the outlaws I see in my dreams." Though different songs, both are united in their love for this "great Southwest."

Other Inanimate Symbols

☞ One look at Arizona's state flag and it's no surprise that the state's official colors are blue and gold. They were officially chosen in 1915.

☞ Arizona is the only state with an official necktie: the bolo tie. *Bola* is Spanish for "ball," and South American gauchos (cowboys) used a *bolas* to lasso cattle—the thrown rope's weighted ends would wrap around a cow's legs. In the bolo tie, the thin, woven strap of leather is gathered by a silver clasp. It's such a characteristic of the area that in 1971 Arizona named the bolo tie its official neckwear.

☞ The greenish blue or robin's egg blue of the semi-precious stone turquoise is about as well known a state symbol as Arizona's hours of endless sunshine. It was chosen as the state's official gemstone in 1974.

DID YOU KNOW?

Turquoise got its name in the 16th century, from the French belief that the mineral came exclusively from Turkey—*Turquois*. That was wrong, as there neither was nor is any turquoise in Turkey; but it's common in Arizona, which leads the nation in turquoise production.

The State's Plates

In 1917 Arizona became the first state ever to issue license plates with a pictorial graphic: a black steer head on a white plate, between the state name and the numbers and letters, also in black. The current graphic plate, in use since 1996, shows a saguaro on the left and Four Peaks, in purple, in the background. You can easily see the real Four Peaks by looking east from Phoenix. Special-issue plates are also common in Arizona, some requiring special qualifications, while the fees of others are earmarked to fund favorite interests:

☞ Amateur Radio

☞ Child Abuse Prevention

☞ Environmental

☞ Firefighter

☞ Fraternal Order of Police

☞ Hearing Impaired

- ☛ Honorary Foreign Consul
- ☛ Legion of Valor
- ☛ Medal of Honor
- ☛ National Guard
- ☛ Permanent Disability
- ☛ Purple Heart
- ☛ Survivor Former Prisoner of War
- ☛ Veteran Pearl Harbor

LIVING (OR PREVIOUSLY LIVING) STATE SYMBOLS

A Flower by Any Other Name

Before Arizona even became a state in 1912, the saguaro cactus (originally spelled "sahuara") was recognized. On March 18, 1901, the gorgeous, flute-shaped flower was named the official flower of the Arizona Territory. The distinction wasn't made official until long after Arizona entered statehood, but on March 16, 1931, the Arizona State Legislature made it official.

The State Fossil—From the Black Forest

A conifer that towered 200 feet high once flourished in northeast Arizona in what is now called the Black Forest, a region in the Petrified Forest National Park. The tree, related to the redwood, is now red stone: *Araucarioxylon arizonicum,* the state fossil of Arizona. The fossils frequently show boreholes of prehistoric insects and sometimes fossilized beehives.

State Butterfly

There are 550 species of swallowtail butterfly in the world, and one of them, the two-tailed swallowtail, is Arizona's official butterfly. The name comes from the two long, thin extensions on the hind wings that resemble the forked tail of a swallow in flight.

A Crafty Little Bird

The crafty cactus wren doesn't usually grow any larger than about 7 or 8 inches long and is a busy bird indeed. Although it builds a permanent nest, it also builds several others as decoys. The male cactus wren helps the female build these nests, using dry grasses and found feathers, and even weaving in strips of discarded cloth or paper. The female lays three to five eggs that hatch in 16 days, after which the young fledge in another 20 days. The cactus wren was chosen as the state bird in 1931.

State Trout

Rainbow, brook, cutthroat, and brown trout are all to be found in Arizona streams and lakes, but all those species were introduced. The state's only two native species are the Gila trout and the Apache trout, which is Arizona's official fish. (Fishing records for the Apache trout and many other species are listed in the section on Sports.)

State Rattlesnake

Rare and rarely seen, Willard's rattlesnake, also called the Ridge-nose rattlesnake, is small, never longer than 24 inches, and is shy—rather than rattle its tail in warning, it will remain perfectly still and hope you don't see it. You probably won't, in the wild—it lives only in the extreme southeastern part of Arizona, and only in forests above 5500 feet and below 9000 feet. But seeing one is worth it, because it is North America's most gorgeous rattlesnake, its color scheme an intricate pattern of chocolate brown, sepia, russet brown, orange, lavender, pink, cream, white, and black. You can see live Willard's rattlesnakes—Arizona's state rattler—at the Phoenix Zoo and at the Arizona-Sonora Desert Museum near Tucson.

Official Amphibian

Arizona came about the naming of its official amphibian in a rather unique way. In 1985 the Arizona Game and Fish Commission hosted an awareness program, encouraging school children from across the state to vote on what they hoped would become four of the state's official symbols: the mammal, reptile, fish and amphibian. The project turned out to be an educational one, as more than 800 species spanning the four categories were studied. In each case, possible candidates were short-listed. When it came to the amphibian choices, the Arizona tree frog, the Colorado River toad, the red-spotted toad and the spadefoot toad made the grade. Now it was up to the students to vote. The result found the Arizona tree frog winning with a huge margin with 11,622 votes. The Colorado River toad came in second with 8520 votes, followed by the red-spotted toad at 6346 votes and the spadefoot toad at 3486 votes. The Arizona tree frog received the official designation on August 13, 1986.

Official Raccoon

A member of the raccoon family is Arizona's state mammal: the ringtail. Smaller than a housecat, brown but for its black-and-white-banded tail that's longer than the whole body, the ringtail is common but nocturnal and rarely seen. They eat berries, insects, and rodents. Early Arizona settlers and miners used to keep ringtails as pets, to ensure that their cabins remained mouse-free. Hence the ringtail's other common name: miner's cat. Both the mountains north of Tucson and the mountains northeast of Scottsdale have a popular hiking route called Ringtail Trail.

AVERAGES AND EXTREMES

An Abundance of Climates

There's a reason why retirees (nicknamed "Snowbirds" by the young and envious who know them) from northern climes make their way to Arizona for the colder, winter months: it's warm down here. In fact, it's so warm that the average daily temperature in January in the southern city of Yuma, for example, ranges from 43°F to 67°F. The interior uplands parts of the state have slightly lower winter temperatures ranging from 14°F to 41°F—for non-Arizonans sitting through a winter deep freeze hovering at the −50°F mark during the latter part of January 2008, those temperatures sound mighty tempting.

"Mild" is the term used to describe Arizona winters, but that's not the only adjective you could use when describing the state's overall climate. There's "varied" (the more mountainous areas are generally cooler than the flat, desert areas), and "dry" (though it's not uncommon for the skies to open wide and even produce flash flooding). Overall, the state usually has two rainy seasons: a monsoon season from June 15 to September 30, and a winter cold front.

Sun People

The Yavapai Indians take their name from *enyaeva* (sun) and *pai* (people).

The Mega-drought

A 60-year drought starting around 1150 AD utterly parched Arizona (and Colorado, New Mexico, Utah and Wyoming) for three generations.

Hot, Hot, Hot

The highest temperature ever recorded in Arizona was 128°F. Lake Havasu City was the hotspot to score that record on June 29, 1994. Lake Havasu City is where the London Bridge now stands; and before he starred in *The Terminator* (1984), *Aliens* (1986) and *Navy SEALS* (1990), actor Michael Biehn grew up there.

DID YOU KNOW?

Before residential air-conditioning became available around 1940, Arizona residents cooled their air with ice blocks, which in the 1880s sold in Phoenix for 6¢ per pound.

Brrr...C-c-c-cold!

Hawley Lake recorded the state's lowest-ever temperature on January 7, 1971. It was a frigid −40°F that day.

No Polar Bears, But...

Sun-blasted Arizona might be the last place you would find Arctic things, but the state actually has a small area of tundra: on the higher slopes of Humphreys Peak, just north of Flagstaff. The Arctic grayling is one of the many game fish found in Arizona's waters.

Let It Snow

It does snow in Arizona—a whole lot in some places. Sunrise Mountain saw 33 feet of snowfall during the winter of 1972, setting the state record for the maximum winter snowfall. The Heber Ranger Station set the record for the largest single day snowfall with 38 inches falling on December 14, 1967. As detailed in the Sports section of this book, skiers have been flocking to Flagstaff's Snowbowl and Arizona's other world-class ski slopes since 1938.

Dreaming of a White Christmas

The greatest Christmas song of all time was written in the heat of an Arizona summer. In 1940, seated beside the swimming pool at the Arizona Biltmore Resort in Phoenix, Irving Berlin wrote "White Christmas." Popularized by Bing Crosby, the song is the top-selling single of all time in any category of music.

SHAKY GROUND

When the Rocks Rock

Earthquakes virtually never occur *in* Arizona, but quakes that occur in California and Mexico are sometimes felt here. According to the U.S. Geological Survey, "No earthquake in recorded history has caused deaths or injuries in Arizona." Still, there have been seismic events that have frightened folks silly. Here are some of the more newsworthy ones:

☛ Arizona's most famous earthquake event occurred in 1887. Its epicenter was almost 200 miles southeast of Tucson, near the town of Bavispe, Mexico. In Tucson, the ground shook enough that buildings cracked, and some were even toppled over.

☛ About 52 earthquakes peppered the state from September 10 to 23, 1910. On September 23 a strong shock hit the northern part of the state, and there were reports that it was "so severe north of the San Francisco Mountains that Indians fled from the region."

☛ Two years later another tremor near the San Francisco Range resulted in a 50-mile-long crack in the earth.

☛ On January 2, 1935, the countryside east of Yuma experienced a tremor. On January 10 of the same year residents at Grand Canyon Village woke when they felt their homes shaking. That earthquake resulted in some damage with cracked walls, and rockslides also were reported. Other aftershocks were felt until January 15.

☛ An earthquake on January 16, 1950, left inch-wide cracks in the earth near the town of Granado. Some of these cracks were as long as 12 feet.

WILD WEATHER

Lightning Strikes—A Lot

Mogollon Rim, which marks the end of low central Arizona and the start of high northern Arizona, has the second-highest incidence of lightning in the United States—only Tampa Bay, Florida, has more lightning. During Arizona's monsoon months, June through September, storms on the Rim can sound like celestial machine-gun fire.

DID YOU KNOW?

Lightning reaches 50,000°F, which is four times hotter than the surface of the sun. So lightning doesn't "break" a tree—in the split-second of the lightning's touch, the water in every cell in the entire tree boils and expands, instantaneously bursting the tree from the inside out. Nearly all wildfires in Arizona (90 percent) are caused by lightning strikes.

Biggest Downpour

Folks in Workman Creek not only saw more rain during a 24-hour period than they ever had, between September 4 and 5, 1970, but it was also more rain than any community in Arizona had ever seen. Workman Creek set a state record with 11.40 inches of rain. Here are a few other rain-centered records:

☛ The largest amount of precipitation to fall in any given year was recorded in Hawley Lake in 1978. The thirsty Arizona earth eagerly soaked up 58.92 inches.

☛ Davis Dam might be the kind of place name that makes you think of water, but it's the Arizona location recording the lowest amount of annual precipitation. The record was set in 1956—only 0.07 inches of precipitation fell that year.

☛ From February 1901 to January 1902, Sentinel didn't report a single drop of heaven-sent moisture. The 352-day dry spell set a historic state record for the most "consecutive days with no measurable precipitation"—the prehistoric state record was the 12th-century mega-drought, for which day-to-day records aren't available.

Worst of the Worst

One of the worst storms ever to hit the state took place in December 1967. Severe winter weather pummeled the entire state. The melting snow and subsequent rainfall produced flooding throughout Arizona. Pima and Santa Cruz counties alone reported $750,000 in damages.

Flash Floods

Because Arizona is typically dry, people don't expect floods, but flash flooding has caused deaths and damage throughout the years. In one example, on July 20, 1970, three people drowned when their vehicle was swept away in a flash flood. Arizona's worst flood occurred in Clifton (Greenlee County) on

December 4, 1906, after 30 continuous hours of rain: 18 people drowned. Safety tip: never camp in a dry watercourse, which can become a raging torrent literally in seconds.

Dust Devils

Quite common in Arizona, dust devils are rotating updrafts, as are tornadoes. Whereas tornadoes are large and attached to storms and deadly, dust devils are small, appear during sunny days and are *usually* harmless. In Tucson on June 20, 1952, a dust devil struck a construction site, and falling debris killed one worker and injured five.

Tornadoes

Tornadoes are rare in Arizona: in the 71 years since 1937, there have been only 63 of them. The worst one hit an Indian village near Tucson on August 27, 1964, killing two people—the first recorded tornado deaths in Arizona—and injuring nine.

Microbursts

Arizona does not get hurricanes, but hurricane-force winds (faster than 75 miles per hour) can indeed hit—vertically. A column of air less than 2.5 miles wide rushing from the sky straight down at the earth is a called microburst. They're not common in Arizona, but microbursts do occur and can cause tremendous damage, because the air column is moving so fast. On August 14, 1996, a microburst moving at 115 miles per hour plunged straight down onto a small area in the northern part of Phoenix and caused $160 million in damage.

Dust Storms

A serious driving hazard occurs in Arizona, especially between June and September, when strong winds suck up dirt and create a wall of dust that can be many miles wide and thousands of feet tall. In the Sahara, a similar wall of sand is called a *haboob*. On April 9, 1995, a dust storm near the town of Bowie, Arizona, hit Interstate 10 and caused four separate vehicle accidents that killed 10 people and injured 20. That same storm ripped the roof off a bank building in Scottsdale.

THE LAY OF THE LAND

Who Owns What

Of Arizona's total land area, 15 percent is privately owned, Native American lands account for 28 percent of Arizona's area, and public lands, forests, parklands, recreation areas make up the remaining 57 percent.

The Grand Canyon State is not a small state compared to other regions:

Region	Square miles
Arizona	113,998
Ecuador	109,484
New Zealand	104,454
United Kingdom	93,784
Syria	71,498
Massachusetts	10,555

Arizona measures about 400 miles from its northern to its southern borders, and about 310 miles from west to east. It shares a 389-mile border with the Mexican states of Sonora and Baja California, and its five American neighbors are New Mexico, Colorado, Utah, Nevada and California.

Three Important Points

☞ The original land survey point for all of what later became the State of Arizona is west of Phoenix in Avondale, atop the hill near the confluence of the Gila and Salt rivers—today home of the Phoenix International Raceway.

☞ Mosey on down about 55 miles east-southeast from Prescott, in Yavapai County, and you'll find yourself at the geographic center of Arizona.

☞ The only place in the United States where four states intersect at one point is Four Corners, where you can walk through Arizona, New Mexico, Utah and Colorado in a few steps. Aside from the marker indicating the four-corner boundary lines of each neighboring state, there isn't much to see. The surrounding desert is barren, and although there are a few vendors offering Native crafts, jewelry and snacks, the nearest place to shop is another six miles away at Teec Nos Pos. So this is really just a photo-op stop, and you'll have to pay for that pretty picture.

The High Points
Take your pick of mountain peaks in Arizona: there are 3928 of them. Yavapai is the most mountainous county, with 426 peaks. Yuma County, with 72, is the least mountainous. The best-known mountain, Camelback, in Maricopa County, is only 2704 feet high. Arizona's highest mountain, Humphreys Peak, in Coconino County, is *now* 12,562 feet high. Before the top of it blew off in prehistoric times, it was in excess of 16,000 feet high. In comparison, Mount Rainier, near Seattle, Washington, is merely 14,411 feet high, and California's Mount Whitney is only 14,505 feet.

Middle Ground
Overall, Arizona's average elevation is 4100 feet above sea level.

Low Point
Where the Colorado River leaves the United States and enters Mexico—after wending its way from its headwaters in Colorado, across Utah and Arizona, and then southward, forming Arizona's border with California—is where you'll find yourself at the lowest elevation in the state: 70 feet above sea level.

Up or Down to Tucson?

The city of Tucson is south of Phoenix, but from Phoenix one drives *up* to Tucson, which is 2389 feet above sea level, compared to Phoenix's elevation of 1117 feet.

WATER, WATER, NOT EVERYWHERE

Arizona: Just Add Water

Of Arizona's total land area, a mere 364 square miles, or about 0.32 percent, is covered by water. But in fact there are lots of lakes, rivers and streams. For example, the White Mountains alone (famous for trout-fishing) have a total of 820 miles of streams.

Major Lakes

There are lots of lakes and reservoirs dotting the landscape here and there throughout Arizona, but most are small and almost pond-like. The six lakes large enough to appear on all maps are Lake Mead, Lake Havasu, Lake Mohave, Lake Powell, San Carlos Lake and Roosevelt Lake. Although relatively small in comparison to large lakes in other states, some of Arizona's lakes made a mark on the country.

☛ Back in 1911 a masonry dam on the Salt River was constructed, leading to the formation of one of the state's largest body of water, Theodore Roosevelt Lake. It's also the oldest artificial reservoir in Arizona.

☛ Named for Dr. Elwood Mead, Lake Mead is the country's largest human-made reservoir. It was basically created with the building of Hoover Dam (completed in 1935) and stretches for about 110 miles behind that monstrous concrete wall.

☛ Unlike most other Arizona lakes, Lake Havasu is fairly substantial. It boasts "more than 400 miles of stunning coastline" at a location that sees more than 300 days of sunshine a year. It's also deeper than most lakes in the state and is dotted with coves and inlets. The lake is home to the bonytail chub and razorback sucker, two of Arizona's endangered native fish populations. *Havasu* is the Indian word for "bluish green."

☛ Lake Mohave is actually a 67-mile portion of the Colorado River and is literally an oasis in an otherwise dry and barren landscape. The long and narrow lake is four miles at its widest point and is bordered by the Pyramid, Painted, Eldorado and Black Canyons. The neatest thing about Lake Mohave is that amid the canyon walls are small, sandy beaches accessible only by boat—a great destination for a little alone time!

☛ The Coolidge Dam, located on the Gila River, is responsible for the creation of San Carlos Lake. It's located right in the middle of the San Carlos Apache Indian Reservation and is considered Arizona's second largest lake.

☛ Both Utah and Arizona boast about the beauty of Lake Powell. Located on their shared border, the lake is formed by a reservoir of the Colorado River and is considered the second largest human-made reservoir in the United States, making Arizona home to the top two in that category. The chiseled walls of Glen Canyon, which surround the lake, makes for absolutely stunning scenery.

Major Rivers

There are four major rivers in Arizona: the Colorado River, the Little Colorado River, the Gila River and the Bill Williams River.

☛ For about 1400 miles, the Colorado River snakes its way through the landscape, but nowhere is its powerful flow more obvious than when it cuts through the Grand Canyon, making its way to the Sea of Cortez. In the early days of this country, engineers tried to divert the flow of the Colorado River in order to use its water for irrigation, but to no avail. The Colorado River has a mind of its own—as it should.

☛ The Little Colorado River, which stretches for about 315 miles, is one of the larger tributaries of the much larger Colorado River. It's been documented to carry as much as 30,000 cubic feet of water per second during rainstorms and can ease off to as little as 150 cubic feet per second during dry spells. On average, though, the Little Colorado River carries about 5200 cubic feet of water per second, draining from the Painted Desert.

☛ The Gila River is another tributary of the Colorado River. It stretches from the southwestern corner of Arizona, near Yuma, for 649 miles across the southern portion of the state and into New Mexico. The Gila River is considered "one of the largest desert rivers in the world," and it flows in a southwesterly direction into the Colorado.

☛ The Bill Williams River winds its way from the Alamo Reservoir to the Colorado River, near the Parker Dam. At a length of 36 miles, it's a relatively short river. It was named after an Arizona mountain man, William S. Williams (1787–1849). The town of Williams (2006 population: 3094), in Coconino County, is also named after him.

Some More Water Trivia

☛ Located in Santa Cruz Valley, south of Casa Grande, and equidistant between Phoenix and Tucson, Arizona City has the purest water in the state—100 percent pure. The state's worst water is in Coconino County at Bitter Springs (2000 population: 547).

☛ Blackwater is a village in Maricopa County, Bluewater is a village in La Paz.

☛ Whiteriver is in Navajo County. Black River is in Maricopa County.

☛ Chinle (Apache County) is a Navajo name meaning "place where water emerges from a canyon's mouth."

☛ State dams and water projects: Bartlett Dam, Central Arizona Project, Coolidge Dam, Glen Canyon Dam, Granite Reef Diversion Dam, Horse Mesa Dam, Horseshoe Dam, Hoover Dam, Mormon Flat Dam, New Waddell Dam, Parker Dam, Roosevelt Dam, Stewart Mountain Dam, Salt River Project.

AMAZING GEOGRAPHICAL FEATURES

Wide, Wild and Wonderful

One of the largest land formations in Arizona is the Colorado Plateau. The pie-shaped portion of the plateau covers one-third of the state, from just north of Arizona's center north and northeast, and extends into Utah, Colorado and New Mexico for a total of about 130,000 square miles. The plateau is called a "physiographic province" by geologists and is unique in its age (estimated at about 500 million years old or older), its weird formations and its vast stretches of flat land. While the landscape around it was reshaping and reforming into the mountains of the Grand Canyon, for example, the Colorado Plateau remained intact. Some sources suggest the entire region is "floating on a cushion of molten rock."

Most Sacred Mountain

Located on the southern border of Metro Phoenix, South Mountain Park, 25.5 square miles, is the largest city park in the United States. But it has a much grander claim to fame: it was the Garden of Eden, where God created mankind, according to Native people's creation story. The Maricopa, Mohave, Yuma and Halchidoma tribes once believed that when he had decided to bring life into existence, the Creator sat down atop Mount Suppoa (at 2690 feet, the highest of South Mountain Park's peaks) and proceeded to do so. Creating humankind first, he watched the people carefully, then used some of them to create animals—a man with a bad temper became Scorpion, a woman who gabbed all the time became Butterfly, a boy who could run fast became Antelope and a man who loved practical jokes became Coyote.

Don't Forget a Gift for God

Inside a different mountain, Baboquivari, 50 miles southwest of Tucson, there is an elaborate cave system in which a god named I'itoi is said to live. According to the Tohono O'odham people, visitors who plan to go inside the labyrinth should leave a gift for I'itoi at the entrance, if they want to find their way back out.

Black Mesa

The largest land feature of the Colorado Plateau is known as the Black Mesa. Reaching a full 8000 feet at its highest point, the Black Mesa is basically a large black mountain sitting in stark contrast to the clay-colored earth of the surrounding plateau. There's a good reason for the dark color—it's full of coal. And since the 1960s, several companies have harvested coal by strip-mining the mountain.

A Hero's Mountain

Hayes Peak, visible to the southwest of Phoenix as the northern-most peak in the Sierra Estrella Mountains, is named after Ira Hayes, one of the U.S. Marines who raised the flag at Iwo Jima. A Pima Indian born in Sacaton, Arizona, Hayes is one of the men immortalized in the famous bronze memorial near Arlington National Cemetery. Of the five flag-raisers, three survived the war—and one of them was Hayes, who died in 1955 at age 32.

Blow Me Away!

About 50,000 years ago, a section of the Colorado Plateau was hit with an impact of such force its landscape was forever altered. The Barringer Meteorite collided with that corner of the world, gouging a crater measuring about one mile in width and 570 feet deep. When European explorers first discovered the area, it wasn't entirely clear what they'd found. Chunks of meteorite were scattered around the rim's depression, and it wasn't until 1891 that Grove Karl Gilbert of the U.S. Geological Survey suggested that the crater was made by a meteorite.

His findings pointed out a "steam explosion" likely created the hole. Daniel Moreau Barringer, a mining engineer who decided to check out the site for himself in 1902, disputed that theory. He hypothesized that it would have taken an extremely large meteorite to make the impression it did, and it would have likely deposited valuable ores and minerals in the process. He supported his theory with five pieces of evidence: the amount of "pulverized silica" at the site could only have been created by the kind of pressure forced on rock by a meteorite; meteoritic iron was found at the site; also found was "the random mixture of meteoritic material and ejected rocks"; the types of rock scattered around the rim were similar to the types of rock layering the crater, but in opposite order; and there was no "naturally occurring volcanic rock" in the area.

In 1908, a geologist named George P. Merrill took Barringer's work further, as did other scientists, such as astronomer A.C. Gifford. The end conclusion was that the "force of an impact at astronomical speeds would result in the explosion of the meteorite," and "whatever the original angle of impact, the result would be a circular crater." Today, scientists believe the meteorite that caused the crater was composed of nickel and iron, measured about 150 feet across and was traveling about 28,600 miles per hour when it made contact—that's equivalent to "150 times the force of the atomic bomb that destroyed Hiroshima."

DID YOU  KNOW?

In the 1984 film *Starman*, the extraterrestrial, played by Jeff
Bridges, goes to Arizona's Meteor Crater to meet his mother
ship. Two decades earlier, after President John F. Kennedy in
1961 announced the goal of putting a man on the moon, NASA
looked around for the best, most barren and lunar-like place to
train its Apollo astronauts—and sent them to the bottom of
Meteor Crater.

A Painter's Palette

There's no doubt behind the naming of Arizona's Painted
Desert. Layers and layers of minerals and organic matter have
compressed and hardened over more than 220 million years,
forming colorful bands of gray, red, orange and yellow on the
endless number of dunes and hills and mesas covering the
93,533 acres that make up this ancient landscape. Visitors can
take in this magnificent natural gem by traveling a 10-mile
length of roadway paved through the park and dotted with
information plaques for ease of access and reference.

World's Grandest Canyon

Let's start with the facts: the Grand Canyon, a gorge primarily
carved by millions of years worth of hammering by the
Colorado River, is about 277 miles long. It's completely con-
tained within the State of Arizona, and it varies in width from 4
to 18 miles. Major John Wesley Powell logged the first recorded
journey into the area in 1869, but he was hardly the first one
there: the Havasupai people have lived in the bottom of the
Grand Canyon for 800 years. The canyon and surrounding
area—about 1902 square miles in total—was one of the first
areas in the country to be named a national park. It was
bestowed with the honor on February 26, 1919.

Although both sides of the Grand Canyon are blow-your-mind amazing, more than 90 percent of the roughly five million visitors make the South Rim their destination of choice. This is because it is easier to access and has numerous hotels, restaurants, museums and shops located nearby. Shuttle buses provide eight-mile excursions of West Rim Drive, there's a 26-mile roadway for the more independent travelers to access with their own vehicles, and a long list of hiking paths and even mule trails is available. The North Rim gives an obviously far different perspective of the canyon, and its hiking trails are a lot more challenging.

DID YOU KNOW?

It was a hiking enthusiast and former U.S. senator from Arizona, Ralph Cameron, and his brother Niles, who supervised the construction of the Bright Angel Trail down into the Grand Canyon, in 1899.

Locked in Time

Each year about 600,000 people check out the petrified wood and search for the remnants of prehistoric plants and creatures etched into the ancient rock of Arizona's Petrified Forest National Park. Located between Holbrook and Navajo, the park boasts the world's largest and most colorful concentrations of petrified wood.

Initially, the Petrified Forest portion of the area received the designation of National Monument on December 8, 1906. Almost 60 years later, on December 9, 1962, the Painted Desert joined the Petrified Forest as a natural wonder worthy of protection, and an area extending about 218,522 acres (or 341.5 square miles) was made into a national park.

Along with the area's natural beauty, a visit to the Agate House, a building constructed out of petrified wood by the Puebloan people, is a definite must. The eight-room home looks a little like a stack-wall house, with squares or cubes of petrified wood stacked from ground to ceiling, and the interior of the house contains an assortment of Puebloan artifacts dating back to the Pueblo III Period, sometime between 1150 and 1350 AD.

DID YOU  KNOW?

When President Franklin Delano Roosevelt asked him why he was always stressing the need for roads and highways, Arizona Senator Carl Hayden replied, "Because Arizona has two things people will drive thousands of miles to see, the Grand Canyon and the Petrified Forest, and they can't get there without roads."

The Arizona Strip

The part of the state north of the Grand Canyon is called the Arizona Strip. Its 7878 square miles is only 6.9 percent of the state's area—but is still larger than, for example, the entire state of Connecticut (5543 square miles).

The remoteness and relative inaccessibility of the Strip has made it the home of polygamous communities for more than a century, including Colorado City, where Warren Jeffs led the Fundamentalist Church of Jesus Christ of Latter-day Saints until he was arrested in 2006.

COUNTY CURIOSITIES

Out of Four Came 15

When Abraham Lincoln made Arizona a Union Territory, it had four enormous counties: Pima, Yuma, Mohave and Yavapai. These were ultimately carved up into today's 15. The first county to be carved out was Maricopa, in 1871; the last was La Paz, in 1983. Of Arizona's 15 counties, two have Spanish names (La Paz and Santa Cruz), two have English names (Graham and Greenlee) and 11 have Native American names (Apache, Cochise, Coconino, Gila, Maricopa, Mohave, Navajo, Pima, Pinal, Yavapai and Yuma). Arizona's largest county,

Coconino, is the second largest county in the United States. The Grand Canyon passes through its 11,886,720 acres. Mohave County, with 8,486,400 acres, is the second largest county in Arizona and the third largest in the nation. Arizona's smallest county, 797,240 acres, is Santa Cruz. Here is a little bit of information on each of the 15 counties:

☛ Apache County occupies a long, narrow strip of land along Arizona's eastern border, extending from its northernmost boundaries about two-thirds the way to its southern border. Founded in 1879, Apache County is home to Arizona's Petrified Forest National Park. Actor John Wayne was among its most famous residents.

☛ Cochise County is nestled in the southeast corner of Arizona. Its tourism department calls Cochise County the "Land of Legends," and they've backed up the claim with an endless amount of evidence. Cochise County is home to Tombstone and the O.K. Corral, the San Pedro Riparian National Conservation Area and its Kartchner Caverns— "one of the top 10 living caves in the world"—and an endless list of hikes suited to beginners and advanced hikers and everyone in-between.

☛ Almost 30 percent of the population of Coconino County is made up of Native American peoples. Most of these individuals are Navajo, Havasupai or Hopi.

☛ According to 2006 U.S. Census estimates, there are about 52,209 people living in the 4796 square miles that make up Gila County, giving it a population density of only about 10 persons per square mile.

☛ Graham County shares its borders with more counties than any other in Arizona. Its neighbors are Cochise, Pima, Pinal, Gila, Navajo, Apache and Greenlee counties.

☛ Greenlee County was formed on March 10, 1909, making it the state's 14th county.

☛ La Paz County is named for the Spanish word meaning "peace." It was founded in 1983, making it the 15th and last county to form in Arizona.

☛ With a population, according to 2006 U.S. Census estimates, of 3,768123 residents, Maricopa County is considered more populated than 23 entire states. More than half of Arizona's residents live there.

☛ Mohave County is located on the western boundary of the state, stretching from Arizona's northernmost portion south until just below its center.

☛ Women in Pinal County seem to have the pick of the litter when it comes to finding a male partner. That's because according to the 2000 Census, for every 100 females in Pinal County, there are 114.20 males.

☛ Navajo County was formed in 1895, and about 66 percent of the 9949 square miles forming the county is "Indian reservation land."

☛ Pima County is one of Arizona's four founding counties. It was formed in 1864. Pima's major city is Tucson.

☛ Folks in Santa Cruz County are proud to boast that good things come in small packages. About 43,080 people (according to 2006 U.S. Census estimates) call Arizona's smallest county home. The county was named after the Spanish phrase for "holy cross."

☛ Yavapai County was the political center of the Arizona Territory, with Prescott as the territorial capital.

☛ Another of Arizona's four founding counties, Yuma County was formed on November 9, 1864. It wasn't until 1983, with the formation of La Paz County, that any changes were made to Yuma's boundaries.

DID YOU KNOW?

Arizona once had a Pah-Ute County. Located in the northwestern corner of the state, Pah-Ute County was formed in 1865, but in 1866 the portion of the county located west of the Colorado River became part of Nevada and the rest was annexed by Mohave County.

PREHISTORIC ANIMALS

Arizona's Longest Ruler was Canadian

A "Canadian" ruled the land of Arizona for many thousands of years. Named after Alberta, Canada, where bones of the species were first discovered in 1884, *Albertosaurus sarcophagus* was a close relative of *T. rex*. At the top of the food chain on the land of Arizona, the albertosaur grew to 30 feet long and ran like an elephant. At the top of the food chain in Arizona's waters was the plesiosaur, a marine reptile that grew to 40 feet long and swam like a sea lion.

The Arizonasaur

Long before the albertosaur and the plesiosaur, the arizonasaur roamed the state. A dinosaur that was closely related to crocodiles, it had a large dorsal fin—a "sail back" of long bones rising from its spine.

PRESENT-DAY WILD LIFE

The Broad Picture

The Arizona landscape today is among the most varied of any state in the nation, and it is populated with a wide array of native (and imported) plant and animal life. The University of Arizona Library estimates there are about 751 vertebrate species—broken down, that number represents 64 species of fish, 22 amphibians, 94 reptiles, 434 birds, and 137 mammals. There are another 20,000 different species of invertebrates, and about 3900 species of native and naturalized plants in the state.

Sounds like an environment teeming with nature, but Arizona is a growing state and that usually means human inhabitants are increasingly encroaching on wild spaces. This is just one of the reasons why some species—one source suggests at least 39 animals and 17 plants—have found themselves on the endangered or threatened list. Some of those animals, such as the jaguar, ocelot, grizzly bear and gray wolf, are among the more familiar species on the list. The lesser long-nosed bat or the Chiricahua leopard frog are perhaps a little more elusive and, therefore, not as recognizable to the general public. The Arizona Game and Fish Department, along with other smaller, not-for-profit groups, are focusing considerable efforts at protecting these and other wildlife so generations yet to be born will have the chance to experience the wonder of it all.

PLANTS

Wildflower Watching

As any subscriber to *Arizona Highways* knows, this state is a treasure house of wildflowers. Strictly speaking, our desert flowers are neither annuals nor perennials, but ephemerals, completing their entire life cycle in just a few weeks. Most germinate only after heavy seasonal rains, and thanks to atmospheric and sun spot cycles, Arizona's wildflowers experience a "super bloom" every 11 years. The next expected super bloom: 2019.

More than Just Cacti

More than a quarter of Arizona's area is covered by forests of oak, aspen, birch, spruce, fir and pine—including the largest stands of ponderosa pine in the United States. (The ponderosa pine was named from the word "ponderous," because the trees reminded early explorers of elephant legs.)

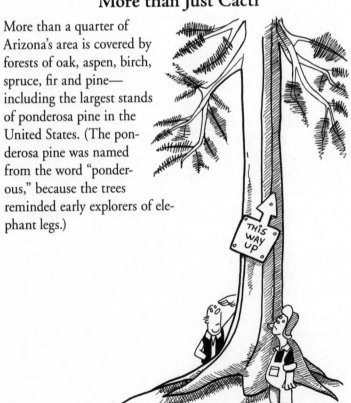

THIS WAY UP

Forests and Parks

Arizona boasts has 31 state parks and six national forests: Apache-Sitgreaves, Coconino, Coronado, Kaibab, Prescott and Tonto. Here's a little of what you'll have to look forward to, should you plan a trip to one of these six amazing locations:

☛ Apache-Sitgreaves National Forests cover about two million acres in the east-central part of the state and is actually two parks melded into one. As one unit, you can find about 34 lakes and reservoirs and more than 680 miles of rivers and streams in this lush, green wilderness, but each park also boasts its own main attractions. The Mongollon Rim stretches for about 200 miles from Yavapai County to New Mexico. The rocky ridge rises about 3000 feet from the valley floor and is a major feature of the Sitgreaves portion of the park. Some of lakes located in the Apache Forest are well known for their great trout-fishing.

☛ Located more centrally than the Apache-Sitgreaves National Forests, the Coconino National Forest still occupies almost two million acres of its own. Perhaps its largest claim to fame (quite literally) is Humphreys Peak, the highest peak in the state. That by no means takes away from the majesty of the Red Rock region near Sedona. Wind-sculpted, orange and red sandstone cliffs have captured the imagination of artists, photographers, writers and moviemakers from around the world.

☛ There are 12 separate mountain ranges in the 1.78 million acres making up the Coronado National Forest in southeastern Arizona.

☛ The Kaibab National Forest is in Arizona's southwestern region. Aside from its natural beauty, the park is home to the largest contiguous ponderosa pine forest in the country. "Kaibab" stems from a Paiute word meaning "mountain laying down."

☛ The Prescott National Forest, consisting of 1.25 million acres, borders the Kaibab, Coconino and Tonto forests, and was first established as the Prescott Forest Reserve on May 10, 1898. It acquired its current name in 1908 after absorbing the Verde National Forest into its boundaries.

☛ At almost three million acres, the Tonto National Forest is the largest in the state and fifth largest in the country. About 5.8 million visitors venture there each year, checking out the many canyons or fishing in one of its six human-made lakes. Along with the natural wildlife roaming the area, about 26,000 cattle are allowed to graze the forest.

The Idiot Forest

Tonto National Forest actually means "Idiot National Forest." Near the geographical center of Arizona, the forest gave its name to Tonto, the Lone Ranger's faithful companion. Because *tonto* means "idiot" in Spanish, Portuguese and Italian, episodes dubbed in those languages changed his name to Toro ("bull"). For the same reason, the Tonto Apache tribe (140 members in 1994), long ago called idiots for their willingness to live peaceably near white men, prefer to call themselves the Dilzhe'eh Apache, which means "people with high-pitched voices." The earliest use of the name "Apache" dates from 1581, when members of the Espejo Expedition referred to the "Apichi" Indians. During the 19th century, a great many European tourists came to Arizona to experience the Wild West, including French people, and today, *apache* is French slang for "ruffian" or "thug."

Arizona's Jungle

Fossil Springs Wilderness is an 11,550-acre area located at the bottom of a steep-walled, 1600-foot-deep canyon where a natural spring pumps to the surface at the rate of about 20,000 gallons per minute. This water supply supports one of the most diverse riparian ecosystems in Arizona, with more than 30 species of trees, numerous broad-leaf tropical plants and abundant wildlife, including more than 100 species of birds. Fossil Springs is 30 miles east of Camp Verde and 86 miles south of Flagstaff, reached by steep gravel roads, followed by a five-mile hike.

Mesquite Trees

The deciduous mesquite tree is the most common small tree in the Arizona desert. There are three varieties of these trees with tiny fern-like leaves: the velvet mesquite, the honey mesquite and the screwbean mesquite. Of these, the velvet mesquite, often known as "native" or "Arizona" mesquite tree, is perhaps the most commonly found throughout arid regions of the state, especially in the Sonora Desert. Root systems can penetrate the earth as far as 175 feet in search of water, which certainly helps when it comes to living in such a dry environment. Although mesquites are categorized as small trees or even shrubs, they commonly reach heights of 15 feet. Along with their yellow-green flowers, the velvet mesquite—which is a member of the legume family—produces bean pods that when fully developed can measure 8 inches long. These pods are a crucial food source for area wildlife—about 80 percent of a coyote's diet is made up of these pods.

Our Single Palm

Palm trees are so ubiquitous in Arizona that it's startling to realize that only one of them is a native species: the Arizona fan palm, scientifically named after George Washington, *Washingtonia filifera*. Some of the palm trees standing in Arizona today were alive when the Father of Our Country was—the Arizona fan palm can live 250 years.

King of the Cacti

The world's biggest cactus, the saguaro (pronounced "sah-wah-roh"), can exceed 52 feet high and can weigh more than 12 tons. They can grow as many as 50 arm-like branches, but the first branch doesn't appear until the saguaro is 75 years old. Some saguaro standing in Arizona today are older than

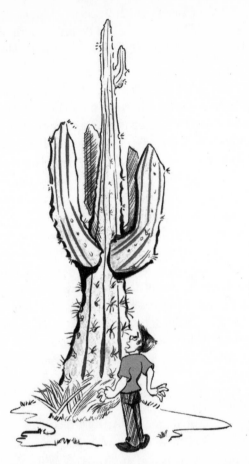

America—saguaros can live more than 200 years. They grow nowhere in the world except the Great Sonoran Desert, which extends from Mexico to Central Arizona. The saguaro flower—Arizona's official state flower—blooms between April and June. A single saguaro can have as many as 200 blooms that take turns opening from night to night and close up around noon of the next day. The saguaro produces an oval-shaped green-colored fruit with red flesh that is food for many desert species, including people.

Other Prickly Friends

Being a partially desert state, it's no surprise that many other types of cacti are found in Arizona. Here are some of the more prolific varieties:

☞ Prickly pear cactus—a flat-padded, sharp-spined cactus that grows to a height of about seven feet and has bright-yellow blossoms. It also produces an edible fruit that along with the pulp from the pads, is used to make prickly pear nectar.

☞ Organ pipe cactus—the only place you'll find this multi-pronged cactus is in a portion of the Sonora Desert, stretching from southwestern Arizona to Sonora, Mexico. This cactus can reach a height of 23 feet and boasts lavender-colored flowers on its tips.

☞ Cholla ("choy-ah") cactus—this family is the most common one in Arizona, with more than 20 species.

☞ Barrel cactus—named for its barrel shape. The flowers topping it are either yellow-green or red and were traditionally boiled and eaten by Native Americans.

Two Desert Survival Tips
☞ The barrel cactus can help you find your way home if you get lost in the desert. Because it almost always grows or leans toward the south, it is sometimes called the "compass cactus."

☞ And contrary to popular belief, barrel cacti are not filled with water. Drinking their highly alkaline juice can cause dehydration, diarrhea and, surprisingly, as your body temperature drops, hypothermia.

Some Places Named for Plants

Strawberry (Gila County) was named for its wild strawberries. Other Arizona towns named for plants include Ash Fork (ash trees), Oak Creek (plentiful oaks), Cottonwood (16 huge cottonwood trees that stood there in 1874), Chino Valley (from *de china*, Spanish for "grama grass"), Sahuarita (saguaros), Green Valley (grassy meadows), Nogales (Spanish for "walnut tree") and Ajo (Spanish for "garlic"). However, Cornville (Yavapai County) had nothing to do with corn—the town's name originated from a typo. Verde Valley pioneers decided to name their new town Cohnville, to honor the Cohn family. When the official papers came back from Washington, DC, some bureaucrat had typed it as "Cornville."

ANIMALS

Butterflies Galore

With 334 species, Arizona has a greater diversity of butterflies than any other state except Texas. Why don't we ever see butterflies at dawn? Because butterflies cannot fly if their body temperature is less than 86°F.

The Great Tarantula Migration

Once each year, in the early summer mating season, millions of tarantulas in southern Arizona come together and for several miles move like a gigantic bear rug being dragged across the desert. All spiders have venom, but the tarantula's is so mild that its bite is harmless to humans.

DID YOU  KNOW?

All Arizona's spiders, scorpions and centipedes, 26 percent of its snakes and one of its lizards, have venom—the chief function of which is not to kill but to rapidly break down the cells of its prey to aid digestion.

Most Dangerous Creatures

Statistically, Arizona's scorpions are far more dangerous than its rattlesnakes. Around 150 people in the state are bitten by rattlesnakes each year, compared to approximately 7000 people stung by scorpions. Although fatalities are extremely rare from either the reptile or the arachnid, scorpions kill more people. From 1929 to 1954, there were 69 scorpion fatalities in Arizona—compared to Arizona's average of one rattlesnake fatality per year.

And the Scorpion Crown Goes to...

Fourteen states in the U.S. each have only one species of scorpion. In contrast, Colorado has seven species, Texas and New Mexico each have 16 species of scorpion, and Nevada has 23. And Arizona? A whopping 42 species of scorpion, all nocturnal. But the scorpion crown is worn by California, which has 59 species. Incidentally, scorpions don't have tails—the long and highly flexible abdomen merely resembles a tail.

Monster Toad

The largest toad in North America, the Colorado River toad, is common in central Arizona near water. Its body is almost the size of a football, and this toad can actually catch and eat mice. Like all toads, it secrets a toxic liquid from two kidney-bean-shaped lumps on its back behind each eye. This substance can kill a dog and is hallucinogenic to humans—hence the dangerous custom among certain Arizona teens of "toad-licking."

Arizona is also a Snake

Arizona elegans, the glossy snake, is small and harmless. The genus *Arizona* has only one species and nine subspecies.

Rattlesnake Haven

If you suffer from ophidiophobia (the fear of snakes), then the Grand Canyon State has good news and bad news. The bad news is that Arizona has 73 species of snake, including 18 different kinds of rattlesnake, more than any other state or province in North America. The good news is that encounters with rattlesnakes are not common, bites are rare, most species' venom is weak, similar to a bee's sting, and deaths are virtually unheard of—possibly one per year, compared to, for example, the 1177 people killed in vehicle accidents in Arizona in 2005. All that said, it's best not to encounter, much less tangle with, these Arizona rattlers:

☛ Arizona black rattlesnake

- banded rock rattlesnake

- black-tailed rattlesnake

- Colorado sidewinder, Mojave ("moh-ha-vee") sidewinder and Sonoran sidewinder (each of the sidewinders have a horn-like scale above each eye that gives the sidewinders quite the devilish look)

- desert massasauga rattlesnake

- Grand Canyon rattlesnake (found only in the Grand Canyon)

- Great Basin rattlesnake

- Hopi rattlesnake

- Mojave rattlesnake

- prairie rattlesnake (used by the Hopi in their traditional dances)

- speckled rattlesnake

- tiger rattlesnake

- twin-spotted rattlesnake

- western diamondback rattlesnake

- western rattlesnake

- Willard's rattlesnake (also called the ridge-nosed rattlesnake—Arizona's official state rattlesnake)

Arizona's Deadliest Snake is Harmless

The Arizona coral snake has venom as potent as a cobra's. But the snake's head is as tiny as a newborn human baby's pinkie fingernail, its fangs are miniscule, and there is no record of an Arizona coral snake being able to open its mouth wide enough to latch onto a person, much less any record of a death.

Leaping Lizards!

Venomous snakes aren't the only reptiles to make Arizona their home. At just a little over a foot in length, a full-grown Gila monster makes up for its smallness with its ferocity. Typically dark-skinned with bright pink patches, the Gila monster's "warty" skin isn't its only unique feature—it also has a thick, forked tongue. One of the only two venomous lizards in the world (the other being its close cousin, the Mexican beaded lizard), the Gila monster uses its powerful jaws to capture its prey, then flips itself upside-down. It must do this so that its venom, which sits in its lower jaw, can drain down into the puncture wounds made by the teeth. The Gila monster is a state-protected species.

Horny Toads

Arizona has seven species of horned lizard, popularly called horny toads. When severely threatened, the horny toad squirts blood from its eyes.

Bison Cubed

The only creature on earth whose genus name, species name and common name are all the same word is *Bison bison*, the bison. Not native to Arizona, bison have been here since 1906, when Charles Jesse "Buffalo" Jones drove a herd of 56 animals down from Utah. In Arizona, a cross between a bison and a dairy cow is called a "cattalo."

Imported Elk

Like bison, elk were in danger of becoming extinct in the United States. But in February 1913, just after Arizona became a state, 83 elk were shipped from Yellowstone National Park and released in Cabin Draw near Chevelon Creek (45 miles south of Winslow). From these Wyoming transplants, the Arizona elk population has grown to nearly 40,000.

Javelina, You Say?

This game animal is fairly new to Arizona. Researchers believe the javelina ("ha-va-lee-na") migrated north to Arizona from Argentina, attracted by the brush-type vegetation found throughout the state. Although it looks a little like a wild pig, a javelina is closely related to the European boar. Also called the peccary or the wild pig, this animal is unique to Arizona, Texas and Mexico, and about 60,000 are thought to inhabit about 34 percent of Arizona. A full-grown javelina weighs between 35 and 60 pounds, and they tend to travel in packs of as many as 20 animals. If cornered, they are ferocious and dangerous.

Going Batty?

All together, there are about 1000 species of bats on earth, meaning that about one of every four kinds of mammal on the planet is a bat. Of that immense total, only 46 different species live in North America—28 of which make Arizona their home for part of the year:

Allen's big-eared bat	Mexican free-tailed bat
Arizona myotis	Mexican long-tongued bat
big brown bat	pale Townsend's big-eared bat
California leaf-nosed bat	pallid bat
California myotis	pocketed free-tailed bat
cave myotis	silver-haired bat
fringed myotis	southwestern myotis
ghost-faced bat	spotted bat
greater western mastiff bat	western pipistrelle
hoary bat	western small-footed myotis
lesser long-nosed bat	western yellow bat
long-eared myotis	Yuma myotis
long-legged myotis	

Best Pest Exterminators

The lesser long-nosed bat and the Mexican long-tongued bat eat the nectar of the saguaro and organ pipe cactus as well as other nectar sources and fruit, but Arizona's other 26 species of bat eat *tons* of insects every night. Above a single Arizona city, Scottsdale, bats eat roughly 3000 pounds of bugs each evening.

A Bunch of Chipmunks

Arizona's six chipmunks are the cliff chipmunk, Colorado chipmunk, gray-collared chipmunk, Hopi chipmunk, least chipmunk and Uinta chipmunk.

Only Near the Grand Canyon

The only place on earth to see a Kaibab squirrel is in an area 20 miles by 40 miles on the North Rim of Grand Canyon National Park. This tassel-eared creature's habitat is now officially the Kaibab Squirrel National Natural Landmark.

Know Your Feline Neighbors

Living in Arizona means getting used to living alongside wildlife, and if you know what to expect, it's a generally good relationship. Take the bobcat, for example. Arizona is widely populated by bobcats, and they're nobody's fool when it comes to foraging for food. It's not uncommon for bobcats to live on the outskirts of urban areas. Yet despite their proximity to their human neighbors, they rarely attack people. In fact, if a bobcat does attack, there's a good chance it has rabies.

Mountain lions, however, are a different story. These big cats are shy and prefer to live in mountainous and rocky areas, farther away from human contact. Though a rare occurrence, mountain lions have been known to attack humans. An estimated 3000 mountain lions make their home in Arizona. Besides it and the bobcat, Arizona is home to three other large felines: ocelot, jaguarundi and jaguar.

Wild Mascots

The wildcat, mascot of the University of Arizona, is a native of Europe, Asia and Africa, and it is not found in North America. When the Arizona contingent went to Cuba in 1898 to fight in the Spanish American War, they took with them a mountain lion and a bear as mascots, which were donated by Robert Brow, proprietor of The Palace Saloon in Prescott.

Where the Deer and Antelope Roam

Arizona has two species of deer, the mule deer and the white-tailed deer (a.k.a. the Arizona coues deer), and one antelope, the pronghorn. Deer and antelope are different animals—the pronghorn's closest relative is the giraffe. One obvious difference is that deer have *antlers,* which are shed each year, while antelope have *horns* that they keep their whole lives.

Arizona's pronghorn is by far the best runner on earth. Whereas a cheetah can reach 70 miles per hour and is exhausted after 100 yards, a pronghorn can move at 60 miles per hour for many miles and cruise at 30 miles per hour for hours on end. In comparison, champion thoroughbred racehorses run at only 25 miles per hour. But pronghorns can't jump—if they encounter a fence, they will stop and crawl under it. Pronghorns typically give birth to twins. The newborns can walk in less than an hour, and at four days old they can outrun a human.

Sheep Named for Canada

The wild sheep named for Canada, *Ovis canadensis,* the desert bighorn sheep, is uniquely adapted to life in Arizona: it can go without water for several months, sustaining itself by getting moisture from the plants it eats. But it barely survived contact with non-Native hunters. In 1936, when fewer than 150 bighorn sheep remained, the Arizona Boy Scouts conducted a statewide campaign to save the species from extinction. When the boys' effort was supported by the Isaac Walton League, the Audubon Society and the National Wildlife Federation, President

Franklin Roosevelt in 1939 signed a proclamation creating two Arizona refuges for the species, both of them in Yuma County. The Cabeza Prieta National Wildlife Refuge is 1344 square miles, and the Kofa National Wildlife Refuge is slightly smaller, at 1040 square miles. "Kofa" stands for King of Arizona, the name of an old gold mine there. By 1993 there were about 6000 sheep, and the desert bighorn sheep is now the official mascot of the Arizona Boy Scouts.

The *Real* Hummers

Arizona boasts 18 species of hummingbirds, and 15 of them are found in Sierra Vista (Cochise County), where their abundance ranks that town as "the hummingbird capital of North America." Four species are also widespread throughout the state: Costa's, Anna's, black-chinned and broad-tailed. Hummingbirds serve the vital role of pollinating many of Arizona's flowers, including the bright red blossoms of the Arizona firecracker (*Ipomopsis arizonica*)—which explains why so many humming-bird feeders are made to resemble this bright red flower.

For the Birds

The Tucson Bird Count (TBC) has been held every spring since 2001. One of the largest urban biological monitoring programs in the world, the TBC is a community-based program that monitors bird populations in 1000 sites in and around Metro Tucson. In 2005 the TBC recorded 192,000 individual birds belonging to 212 different species, of which 115 were native and 97 were migratory species. The capital of Canada began its own monitoring program in 2007, the Ottawa Breeding Bird Count, based on the Tucson model.

Beep Beep!

Thanks to Wile E. Coyote's attempts to catch a cartoon one, everyone has heard of the roadrunner. Here's some Arizona roadrunner trivia you may not have heard. Roadrunners don't beep like little cars—they coo, just like doves. They can fly, but prefer to run—at 15 miles per hour. They are large birds, up to 22 inches long—but in prehistoric times, Arizona had a much larger species, the Conkling's roadrunner. Like parrots and woodpeckers, the roadrunner is a zygodactyl: the four toes are arranged in pairs, with the second and third toes in front, and the fourth and the first one (called the hallux), behind.

DID YOU KNOW?

The tarantula hawk (the official state insect of New Mexico) is a large wasp that hunts tarantulas, and because its sting is so excruciatingly painful, no other species feeds on the tarantula hawk—except the roadrunner.

Bald Eagles

In 2007, all of the nation's bald eagles were taken off the Endangered Species list, but on March 7, 2008, a federal judge put Arizona's bald eagles back on the list—there are only 50 nesting pairs in Arizona. Since 1978, the state has had an Arizona Bald Eagle Nestwatch Program.

Best Viewing Sites

Many Arizona animals are nocturnal or rare, and many Arizona plants are remote—but you can see most of them near the state's two biggest cities.

☛ The best place to see Arizona animals—2744 live ones representing 320 species, plus 2068 fossils—is at the Arizona-Sonora Desert Museum, about 15 miles west of downtown Tucson. Opened in 1952, the museum was one of the first naturalistic zoos in the United States. Endangered species you can see there include the Mexican wolf, thick-billed parrot, ocelot, margay, jaguarundi, desert pupfish, Sonora chub, bonytail chub, razorback sucker, Gila topminnow, Colorado River squawfish, Isla San Esteban chuckwalla and Apache trout.

☛ The best place to see Arizona plants—more than 22,000 live cacti, agave and other species, including 140 rare or endangered ones—is at the Desert Botanical Garden, which opened in 1939 in Papago Park, on the border between Phoenix and Scottsdale. The garden's research program focuses on conservation biology (the human impact on plants and environments); ecology (the relationship between organisms and their environment); ethnobotany (the past and present interrelationships of plants and people); floristics (the different kinds of plants within an area); horticulture (growing and using plants in urban settings); and systematics (the origin and evolutionary relationships of plants).

☛ The largest and oldest botanical garden in Arizona is the Boyce Thompson Arboretum. Opened in 1925 and now a state park, it's in Superior, near Phoenix. Its 323-acre botanical collection includes a wide range of habitats that can be viewed on a 1.5-mile walking trail.

Really Wild Night Life

For a thrill far more memorable than watching an animal show on TV, try watching an Arizona wild animal show through your windshield. Most of Arizona's animals come out of their hiding places and move around at night, and by driving slowly (around 25 miles per hour) on low-traffic roads away from any urbanized area, between sundown and 10:00 PM, you can see an astonishing array of wild animals. Deer, javalina, bobcats, rabbits, desert mice, kangaroo rats, owls, nighthawks, rattlesnakes, tarantulas, scorpions, and sometimes porcupines and skunks are just a few of the animals you will see in your headlights, and, if you're lucky, mountain lions. Arizona nature-lovers call this "night-hunting," though the only thing you bag is great memories. Upon seeing a creature ahead, you simply ease your vehicle to a stop and watch the animal move past. You are advised to remain in your vehicle with the windows rolled up.

BOOMING AND DIVERSE

Booms from Ore and Air

Arizona does not exactly have a history of slow and steady population growth. As happened in California at Sutter's Mill in 1848 and in the Yukon during the Klondike Gold Rush of 1897, news of an ore discovery in Arizona caused whole towns to spring up almost overnight.

Within three years of the discovery of silver in 1879, Tombstone grew from a single tent to a city of 15,000 that was immediately named the county seat of Cochise County. Arizona's very first boomtown was Gila City (Yuma County). It's a ghost town today (nothing remains of the town site), but Gila City set the precedent that was followed scores of times throughout Arizona history, as described by an eye-witness who arrived when more than 1000 miners had already descended on the new gold-mining camp:

Enterprising men hurried to the spot with barrels of whiskey and billiard tables. Jewish merchants came with ready-made clothing and fancy wares; traders crowded in with wagon-loads of pork and beans, and gamblers came with cards and monte-tables. There was everything in Gila City within a few months but a church and a jail.

But it wasn't gold or copper or any other ore that triggered Arizona's biggest and still ongoing in-migration boom: it was the sudden availability of cool air on demand. Thanks to affordable residential air-conditioning hitting the national market in the early 1950s, Phoenix went from America's 99th largest city in 1940 to its ninth largest in 1990. Cool air, along with everything else that makes Arizona unique and amazing, helps to explain why, in 2007, some 90,000 new residents moved to Arizona from other states—while, in comparison, 263,000 residents left California.

Canadians, Eh?

A great many people who come to Arizona start out from Canada. In 2006, a total of 495,800 Canadians visited Arizona and spent US$428,023,311. That works out to 1358 Canadian visitors per day, spending $1,172,667 every 24 hours. Canada has its own Arizona Office of Tourism, in Toronto.

Famous Canadians who have made their homes in Arizona include comic actor Leslie Nielsen of *Airplane!* (his father was a Mountie); cartoonist Todd McFarlane, creator of *Spawn* and re-designer of *Spiderman* (Todd was born in Calgary); and ice hockey's G.O.A.T. (Greatest Of All Time), Wayne Gretzky.

One, Two, Three...

The population of Arizona in 2000, based on the U.S. Census, was 5,130,632. The 2006 Census estimates put that number at closer to 6,166,318, which represents more than a 20 percent increase. Although it's the sixth largest state, in terms of land area, Arizona is the 16th most populated state with 2.07 percent of the nation's population living here. Spread that number out over the entire state and that's the equivalent of about 45.02 persons per square mile. In comparison, the population density of Canada is 8.7 people per square mile, while the population density of the United States is 77 people per square mile.

Breaking It Down

Generally speaking, the population of Arizona looks something like this:

☛ 7.8 percent are under the age of five.

☛ 26.4 percent are under 18.

☛ 12.8 percent are 65 or older.

☛ There appears to be a 50/50 split between the number of females and males living in Arizona.

☛ About 12.8 percent of the state's population was born outside the United States.

☛ 25.9 percent (2000 U.S. Census) of the population aged five years and older speaks a language other than English at home.

☛ 81 percent of Arizonians aged 25 years and older are high school graduates, bettering the national average by 0.6 percent (2000 U.S. Census).

☛ When it comes to postsecondary education, about 23.5 percent of Arizonians aged 25 years and older have earned their Bachelor's degree or higher. That's a little lower than the national average of 24.4 percent.

☛ Of the population aged five years and older, about 902,252 people have some type of disability.

(Except where noted, the above figures are based on 2006 U.S. Census estimates.)

Ethnic Diversity

According to the U.S. Census Bureau's estimates for 2006, here's how the population of Arizona breaks down:

Race	Percentage of Population
White (non-Hispanic)	59.7
Hispanic or Latino	29.2
Native American and Alaskan Native	4.8
African American	3.8
Asian	2.4
Persons with two or more ethnic backgrounds	1.6

(Note: The Hispanic or Latino category can be of any race, which is why the figures listed may not add up to 100 percent.)

DID YOU  KNOW?

From highest to lowest, the five most prominent ethnic backgrounds in Arizona are Mexican, German, English, Irish and Native American. In Pima County (Tucson), German is the third most-spoken language, after English and Spanish—and before Pima Indian. Residents of Mexican background are listed under the Hispanic or Latino category in the U.S. Census, and of the 1,803,377 in that category, 1,601,082 are Mexican.

Far from the Pacific
Arizona in 2006 was home to 954 people from Tonga (6th largest Tongan population among U.S. states), 2101 people from Guam (8th largest), 1874 people from Samoa (10th largest), and 6733 were Native Hawaiians (8th largest).

Native Land

Arizona has the largest Native American population of any state—275,321 people in 2007. While there are 21 tribal governments, the state has 27 present-day nations or tribes:

Chemehuevi

Chiricahua Apache

Cocopah

Coyotero Apache

Dilzhe'eh Apache
(Tonto)

Halchidhoma

Halyikwamai

Havasupai

Hopi

Hualapai (Walapai)

Kaibab Paiute

Kohuana

Maricopa

Mohave

Navajo

Papago
(Tohono O'odham)

Pascua Yaqui

Pima
(Akimel O'odham)

Pinal Apache

Quahatika

San Carlos Apache

San Juan Southern
Paiute

Sobaipuri

White Mountain
Apache

Yaqui

Yavapai

Yuma (Quechan)

DID YOU KNOW?

No U.S. treaty was ever made with the Maricopa or the Pima, tribes known to have been friendly toward whites. American history's last Indian raid took place in 1913, when a Yaqui force attacked El Paso, Texas.

Lori Piestewa
Private Lori Piestewa ("pee-es-tay-wa"), a Hopi born in Tuba City, Arizona, was killed in Iraq on March 23, 2000. She was the first Native American woman ever to die in combat while serving with the U.S. military. The second highest point in Phoenix (after Camelback Mountain) was called Squaw Peak for 100 years, but it is now officially Piestewa Peak. State Route 51, which skirts that mountain, was also officially named in her honor: Piestewa Parkway.

African American Firsts

A few states have laid claim to Henry Ossian Flipper—Texas and Georgia, for example. But Arizonans are proud that for a time, Flipper made his home in this fair state. Flipper made military history when, in July 1877, he became the first African American ever to graduate from the U.S. Military Academy at West Point. He was just 21 years old at the time. Other African American firsts in Arizona:

☛ Mary Green and her two children arrived from Arkansas and became the first three African American residents of Phoenix in 1868—two years before Jack Swilling actually founded the town.

☛ Corporal Isaiah Mays is buried at the All Souls Cemetery at Arizona State Hospital in Phoenix. Born a slave in Virginia, Mays was a Buffalo Soldier, and for his conduct defending an army pay wagon against masked bandits near Tucson in 1890, he was awarded the Congressional Medal of Honor.

- Arizona ended segregation in its public schools in 1951, three years before the Supreme Court decision.

- In 1992, Arizona became the first state to have a Martin Luther King Jr./Civil Rights Day as a paid state holiday.

Most Populous Cities

The capital city of Arizona is Phoenix, which is also, by far, the most populous city in the state. Counting down from the top spot, here are Arizona's 10 most populous cities, based on 2006 estimates:

City	Population
Phoenix	1,505,265
Tucson	534,685
Mesa	451,360
Glendale	243,540
Scottsdale	237,120
Chandler	235,450
Gilbert	185,030
Tempe	165,890
Peoria	145,135
Surprise	98,140

County Populations

The most populous county in Arizona is Maricopa County. With an estimated 2006 population of 3,792,675, it's more than three times as large as the next most populous county, Pima, which has 981,280 people. The least populated county in the state is Greenlee County with only 8300 people residing there.

DID YOU KNOW?

Arizona prides itself in being the "second-fastest growing state" in the United States—when, that is, it doesn't beat Nevada for the rank of fastest growing.

Population Through the Years

As with many other states in the nation, the largest 10-year increase in population (percentage-wise) in Arizona occurred during the time the state was being settled. In this case it was from 1870 to 1880, when the population increased by 318.7 percent. In terms of actual numbers of people, the largest 10-year increase was between 1990 and 2000, when the population grew by 1,465,404. Here is the historical picture:

Census Year	Population
1860	6482
1870	9658
1880	40,440
1890	88,243
1900	122,931
1930	435,573
1960	1,302,161
1990	3,665,228
2007 (estimate)	6,338,755

The Name Game

According to the Arizona Department of Health Services, the five most popular names for baby boys in 2004 were José, Jacob, Anthony, Daniel and Angel, with 593, 580, 559, 556 and 519 baby boys receiving those names respectively. Emily, Isabella,

Emma, Madison and Ashley were the top five baby girl names with 425, 371, 347, 342 and 337 baby girls receiving those names respectively.

DID YOU  **KNOW?**

Margaret Sanger, founder of the American Birth Control League (now called Planned Parenthood), died in 1966 in Tucson at age 87, just a few months after *Griswold v. Connecticut* legalized birth control for married couples in the United States.

Religious Preferences

Unlike people in many other states, the residents of Arizona who don't lay claim to preferring one religious denomination or another is a fairly large portion of the overall population—3,082,609 people of the state's 5,130,632 people counted in the 2000 Census. According to the Association of Religion Data Archives, here are the more popular religious and/or denominational preferences:

Christian Denomination/Religion	Membership Total
Catholic	974,883
Evangelical Protestant	486,247
Mainline Protestant	222,305
Orthodox	11,143
Other	353,445

DID YOU  KNOW?

The Church of Scientology began in Arizona after L. Ron Hubbard in March 1952 moved to Phoenix, "the Birthplace of Scientology."

Mormonism

Stereotypes based on extremists have sometimes given the LDS Church (Latter-day Saints) a bad name, but the truth is that Mormonism's core values of family, community, freedom and industry were major factors in the development of Arizona as a great place to live. Flagstaff began as one of the first Mormon settlements in Arizona. One of the state's favorite lakes for trout is Mormon Lake, near Flagstaff. Mesa was founded by Mormon pioneers in 1878, a decade after Phoenix was founded. The founders of Mesa were led by Daniel Webster Jones, whose great-granddaughter was Fay Wray, star of *King Kong* (1933). On December 4, 1924, Cassie Pomeroy and 37 Mesa women formed the Mesa Daughters of the Utah Pioneers to honor the many LDS contributions to the state. In 2008 there were approximately 200,000 Mormons in Arizona.

DID YOU KNOW?

In the years after World War I, The Church of Jesus Christ of Latter-day Saints built three major temples: in Mesa, Arizona; in Cardston, Alberta; and in Laie, Hawaii.

First Marriage

Joe Melczer and Hazel Goldberg of Phoenix had scheduled their wedding for the morning of February 14, 1912, but they postponed the ceremony until they got the word that Arizona had become a state, thereby becoming the first couple married in the State of Arizona. Their ring bearer was three-year-old Barry Goldwater, who grew up to be a U.S. senator and the Republican Party's 1964 presidential candidate.

DID YOU KNOW?

In 2006, there were 38,983 marriages in Arizona and 24,272 divorces.

Tying the Knot—Fast

While Yuma Territorial Prison was associated with tying knots around convicts' necks, Yuma after statehood was *the* place where people went to tie the knot, in a marriage chapel. Early Hollywood stars who hopped out of stringent California to get married in laid-back Yuma, which required neither a blood test nor a three-day waiting period (until 1957), included Mary Astor (star of 123 films); John Barrymore (film director and Drew's grandfather); French actor Charles Boyer; Claudette Colbert; Bette Davis; Alice Faye, called "the most famous singing actress in the world"; Louis B. Mayer (the final "M" in MGM); Tom Mix (star of 336 feature films); Gloria Swanson (60 films); and Loretta Young (100 films).

But the record for the number of trips to Arizona for a quick marriage was set by one of America's all-time best-loved comedians, Arthur Stanley Jefferson, better known as Stan Laurel, the thin one of the Laurel and Hardy team: for four of his six marriages, he and his brides-to-be beelined to Yuma.

ROADSIDE ATTRACTIONS

On the Map

There are 22 national monuments, memorials, sites, parks and areas in Arizona:

- Canyon de Chelly ("dee shay") National Monument—Indian villages built between 350 and 1300 AD.

- Casa Grande Ruins National Monument—the largest prehistoric structure in North America.

- Chiricahua National Monument—spectacular rock formations.

- Coronado National Memorial—commemorating the first European exploration of the Southwest, by Francisco Vasquez de Coronado (1540–42), near the point where his expedition entered what is now the United States.

- Fort Bowie National Historic Site—the 1862 fort that was the focal point of the military operations against Geronimo and his band of Chiricahua Apaches.

- Glen Canyon National Recreation Area—contains Lake Powell, which stretches 186 miles along the old Colorado River channel.

- Grand Canyon National Park—world's greatest example of the power of erosion.

- Hohokam Pima National Monument—a 1690-acre site preserving archeological remains of Hohokam culture (not open to the public).

- Hubbell Trading Post National Historic Site—built in 1878, Arizona's oldest continuously operating trading post.

- Lake Mead National Recreation Area—the first national recreation area ever established by an act of Congress.

- Montezuma Castle National Monument—a five-story, 20-room cliff dwelling—one of the best preserved and most easily accessible cliff ruins in North America.

- Navajo National Monument—well-preserved ruins of villages built by Puebloan people around 1300 AD.

- Organ Pipe Cactus National Monument—protecting the organ pipe cactus, a large species rarely found in the United States.

- Petrified Forest National Park—the world's largest concentration of petrified wood.

- Pipe Spring National Monument—a fort and other structures built here by Mormon pioneers.

- Saguaro National Park—protecting the world's largest cactus.

- Sunset Crater National Monument—a volcanic cinder cone formed in 1100 AD.

- Tonto National Monument—well-preserved cliff dwellings built from 1200 to 1400 AD.

- Tumacacori National Historical Park—includes the mission sites of Tumacacori, Guevavi and Calabazas, established by Father Kino, Jesuit priest, in the late 1690s in the northern frontier of New Spain.

- Tuzigoot National Monument—two-story, 110-room structure built between 1100 and 1450 AD.

- Walnut Canyon National Monument—cliff dwellings built in shallow caves under limestone ledges 800 years ago.

- Wupatki National Monument—red sandstone pueblos built in 1065 AD.

DID YOU  **KNOW?**

Most of Arizona does not observe Daylight Savings Time. Only on Navajo lands in Northeastern Arizona do people adjust their watches forward one hour in spring and backward one hour in fall.

More Than Just Burgers

The Burger King in Kayenta serves up a lot more than a great meal. This fast food joint also offers a good dose of Native American history with its Navajo Code Talker display. Navajo Code Talkers came about as a way to develop an unbreakable form of code during the military operations of World War II, and according to the Naval Historical Center in Washington, DC, their services were used in every assault the U.S. Marines conducted in the Pacific from 1942 to 1945.

The Navajo language is extremely complex—and, at the time, was unwritten, without an alphabet or symbols. Unless you were deeply steeped in the language, it was impossible to decipher, and it wasn't just as simple as sending out a Marine to transmit an English message in Navajo from one location to its destination. What they did was translate Navajo words into English and use the first letter of the English word to spell out military terms. In other instances, English words without Navajo equivalents were replaced with symbolic words—a submarine was a *besh-lo* or "iron fish," for example.

About 200 Navajos were recruited to the navy, and one of those individuals was the father of Richard Mike—owner of the Kayenta Burger King. It was in his honor that a special display, honoring the Navajo Code Talkers, was erected, and today everyone who stops by for a burger can avail themselves of a little history lesson as well.

Old as the Hills

Did you know that petrified wood is about 225 million years old? It's also quite beautiful, if you know what you're looking for and how to treat it. Stewart's Petrified Wood shop, located near the Petrified Forest in Holbrook, has been picking, cutting, polishing and selling the product since 1994. That's when Charles Steward, fascinated by the ancient rock, opened his doors and started business.

But that's not the only draw for visitors passing by. In fact, folks who aren't the least bit interested in petrified wood can't help but stroll around the site. Randomly placed here and there are life-sized statues of dinosaurs, carrying on with the prehistoric theme, and they aren't all that welcoming. Some dinosaurs are shown in the process of consuming mannequins that look all too lifelike and mighty bloody. Others are motorized and therefore quite threatening to some folks, but for Stewart, safety comes first—all of his dinosaurs are in penned areas, making for a great (and safe) photo-op. And if all this wasn't enough, the ostrich farm located on-site makes for some interesting viewing. Ostrich eggs and the birds themselves are also on sale there, as well as petrified jewelry set in gold and silver.

Longhorn Bar & Grill

If you're the kind of person for whom atmosphere makes up a big part of your dining experience, then a trip to the Longhorn Bar & Grill is in order. If you drive by the place, located at 28851 South Nogales Highway, in Amado, you might not even realize what's behind the great skull and longhorns framing the entryway of an adobe-style building that looks a little like a large rock. But take a second look and you'll see that what's behind that façade is a roadside refreshment stop serving up beef burgers and more! It's certainly an experience you won't regret trying out.

DID YOU KNOW?

Rustler's Rooste, the restaurant at The Pointe at South Mountain Resort, in Ahwatukee (just south of Phoenix), serves rattlesnake appetizers. It tastes like chicken.

Silent Salute

If you're traveling along Highway 79 South, not too far away from Florence, you'll come across a monument to the silent film star Tom Mix. Mix was born in 1880 and soared to silent film stardom between 1910 and 1935 when he starred in a staggering 336 films. All but nine of these were silent films, but with or without the audio, they still propelled Mix into the category of Hollywood superstar.

The story goes that Mix was driving across Arizona when his car flew into a gully. Witnesses said that even though Mix's aluminum suitcase slammed into his head, he stood up and took a step out of the wreckage before he died. The monument sports an iron horse atop a mound of stones and mortar, and a plaque that reads:

January 6, 1880 – October 12, 1940

in memory of

Tom Mix

whose spirit left his body on this spot and whose characterization and portrayal in life served to better fix memories of the Old West in the minds of living men.

YOU'VE GOT TO SEE THIS

Traces of the First Americans

Many experts consider the Clovis people to have been the first human inhabitants of the New World, the ancestors of all Native people in North and South America. Named after the town of Clovis, New Mexico, where traces of their culture were first discovered in 1932, the Clovis people lived in the southwestern part of this country between 10,000 and 9000 BC. An especially rich archaeological site was discovered in Arizona near Murray Springs, which is near Sierra Vista (Cochise County). From 1967 to 1971 archaeological digs were conducted at what is now known as the Murray Springs Clovis Site, and today visitors are encouraged to walk the same path as the original inhabitants of the area by following several interpretive trails.

You Might Want to Stay Here

Herbert David Lore knew how to capitalize on the beauty of the Painted Desert and the tourist traffic passing by as early as 1924. That's when he built the Stone Tree House—a wayside stop that acquired its name because so much of the construction material used was petrified wood, which was hard as stone. Originally, Lore sold meals, libations and Native American art, and he even provided a bed for the night.

He operated his business for about 12 years, but in 1935 he sold his land to the National Park Service, which included it in the Petrified Forest National Monument. At that point the "inn" ceased to operate as such, but in 2004 the building was renovated, the name was changed to the Painted Desert Inn, and visitors who tour the site today get a real feel for life as it was almost 100 years ago. Sadly, the inn no longer accommodates overnight visitors.

Bisbee's Best

The Bisbee Queen Mine was often referred to as "one of the richest copper mines in history." But the mine's closure in 1975 didn't stop the community from capitalizing on the Queen in a different way. Since 1976, the Queen Mine has been open for tours and an estimated 50,000 people usually do just that every year. Visitors can see the changing house and can descend into the earth where copper was mined from 1877 on. A slicker, helmet and miner's headlamp are all provided, of course. Perhaps the best part of the tour is that the folks who used to work there give the tours, and they usually sprinkle the tour with their own underground tales. It goes without saying that residents of Bisbee are proud of their entire community, so once you're there, make sure to check out the rest of this historic landmark.

Celebrating Sedona

Folks at the Sedona Heritage Museum, located in Uptown Sedona, honor the 350-million year history the area boasts, but that's not where they've placed their focus. Instead, this must-see museum homes in on Sedona's more recent history, remembering the pioneers who migrated and settled there from 1876 to the present. Visitors will learn about the area's apple and peach industries, the almost 100 feature movies filmed in the area (the museum has a room set aside to remember the many actors and actresses involved in these productions), and also how "real cowboys" tamed the land and made their living there.

DID YOU KNOW?

The first movie filmed in Sedona was in 1923 and was a screenplay of Zane Grey's *Call of the Canyon*. The great German surrealist painter Max Ernst lived in Sedona from 1948 to 1953.

The African Experience

So you want to go to Africa, but a trip that far just doesn't fit your budget? Why not check out the Out of Africa Wildlife Park near Camp Verde! More than 400 "wild-by-nature" animals live on 104 acres of Arizona wilderness, roaming freely while still offering the general public a chance to experience these creatures in a natural environment. Among the many animals you might see on one of the safari outings offered by the park are lions, tigers, jaguars, rhinoceros, wildebeests, zebras, giraffes and more than 100 different species of birds. Bengal and Siberian tigers demonstrate the predator-prey experience during the Tiger Splash show, and you can watch as these large cats catch and consume their prey during the Predator Feed show. The Wonders of Wildlife show demonstrates how human caretakers at the preserve interact with some of the animals. You'll also be offered a first-hand view of just how long some of the world's largest snake species can get.

Arizona's "Most Western" Museum

Residents of Wickenburg call their Desert Caballeros Western Museum "Arizona's Most Western Museum," and if you take a few minutes to browse through what they have to offer, it's easy to see why. First off, it's located in a town full of history and surrounded by the natural beauty of the Wild West. Inside the museum, exhibits focus on the life of the cowboy, the bolo tie in all its forms and incarnations, Western art and women of the West.

Visitors to the town don't have to settle for modern hotel accommodations if they don't want to. Instead, they can take a trip back in time and stay at one of three guest ranches designed with special attention to that Western experience. The nearby abandoned Vulture Mine, famous as the site of one of Arizona's "earliest and largest gold strikes," is open for self-guided tours. The town of Wickenburg also boasts architecture of a time long past, and 10 of their downtown buildings are listed on the National Register of Historic Places. You can book a jeep tour of the rugged countryside surrounding the town or, if you prefer, take a horseback ride. And the nearby Hassayampa River Preserve is home to some of the state's most rare and threatened plant and animal life.

SMALL TOWN ODDITIES

Ghostly Claim to Fame

Today, the city of Douglas boasts a population of 14,312, but 100 or so years ago it was just a babe in the woods. It started out as little more than a copper smelter in 1900, with a few homes sprouting up here and there for mine workers and their families. Stan Jones was born there in 1914 and grew up in the shadow of the copper mine he would one day work at, just like most of the boys he'd grown up with. Nothing out of the ordinary so far, but by 1949 a song he wrote, "(Ghost) Riders in the Sky," would add his name to the cowboy songwriters' history books. The song was a hit for singers such as Burl Ives and America's singing cowboy, Gene Autry, who built a movie around Jones' masterpiece.

Knowing Your Opponents

Arizona is far more than just a pretty face, as far as beautiful landscapes go. The unique desert surrounding the city of Dateland is prime growing space for the lush date, and it has also provided a training ground for American troops preparing for terms of service in Iraq. During World War II, Arizona played an even bigger role in preparing soldiers for the sands of North Africa. Created in 1942 and commanded by General George Patton, the Desert Training Center, California-Arizona Maneuver Area (DTC-CAMA), was the largest military training ground in the history of military maneuvers. Ten other training camps were also established in an area stretching from Boulder City, Nevada, to the Mexican border, and from Phoenix, Arizona, to Pomona, California.

Another Kind of Condo

You'll have to call ahead to make sure the trails surrounding this historic landmark are open (they're sometimes closed because of rock falls or other weather issues), but if you get the chance, a visit to the Walnut Canyon National Monument is well worth the effort. More than 700 years ago, early inhabitants of the Flagstaff area carved their homes out of the canyon walls. Trails throughout the area give hikers a chance to view some of these canyon dwellings, and interactive exhibits are on display at the visitor's center. Also nearby is the Sunset Crater Volcano National Monument, a landscape coated with hardened and crusted lava that flowed through the area sometime between 1040 and 1100.

AMAZING ARIZONA The City of Prescott is proud of its community. So much so that folks there can't imagine anyone living anywhere else, and their logo reinforces that—"Welcome to Everybody's Hometown." Meanwhile, the Town of Carefree, just north of Scottsdale, has its own great motto: "Home of Cowboys and Caviar, Where the Old West Meets the New"—and where Town Hall is located at 100 Easy Street.

The Story Behind the Name

When you think about it, "Tombstone" is an unusual name for a town—but it's an unusual town. A prospector named Ed Schieffelin made his way into the area in 1877. During his regular rock-seeking ventures, the members of his group, who were in the area with him for the purpose of scouting Apaches, regularly warned him that "the only stone [he would] find out there [would be his] tombstone." When he discovered silver, he named his first mine "The Tombstone." The town, which also acquired the name, was founded near the mine in 1879.

Each Snowflake Is Unique—Especially This One

With a name like Snowflake (Navajo County), anyone hearing of the Arizona community would expect it must snow there—at least a little. Although it's not uncommon for the community to receive a little dusting of snow now and then, the weather played no part in the town's naming. Instead, it was named after its two Mormon founders: Erastus Snow and William Jordan Flake. The Snowflake Arizona Temple, completed in 2002, is only the second Latter-day Saints temple to be constructed in Arizona. At its completion, the temple, named after the community where it is located, became the 108th and the latest Mormon temple in the world.

RECORD BREAKERS AND AMAZING FIRSTS

Folklore First

Arizona's first "State Balladeer" was Dolan Ellis. Appointed by Governor Sam Goddard in February 1966, Ellis has more than earned that title, having written more than 300 songs about the state he loves and calls home. So committed is Ellis to his art and his beloved Arizona that he had an even broader vision. Ellis imagined a permanent place in the countryside where the heritage and culture of this state "could be performed and preserved." And so in June 1996, he founded a modest version of today's Arizona Folklore Preserve, setting up a stage in a circa 1920s ranch house near Ramsey Canyon. By the time 30 patrons packed their way into the old building the house was full—it was obvious something a lot larger was needed. By 2000 Ellis joined forces with the University of Arizona South, and the current Folklore Center was built on the 15-acre site Ellis originally purchased. Ellis is still active with the center as the artist-in-residence and continues to perform monthly.

First and Oily

You don't have to rely on Italian imports for a great-tasting extra virgin olive oil. When the Queen Creek Olive Mill, a family-owned and -operated olive farm and mill, first opened for business in 2005, it made Arizona history. It's the state's "first working olive farm and mill," and the company boasts it makes "one of the world's finest extra virgin olive oils." The company welcomes visitors and offers tours—and has tons of recipe ideas for use with their product.

A Man's Best Friend

A dog will do just about anything for its master—and a K-9 dog will fight for us all. It's fitting, then, that after a loyal and long-standing K-9 member of the Gilbert Police Department died in 2002, the community wanted to do something special to commemorate the dog. The German shepherd Cosmo was the first K-9 officer to serve on the force, and she spent six years apprehending criminals and "seizing more than 2000 pounds of illegal drugs." Cosmo will be forever remembered whenever residents of Gilbert take a stroll through Cosmo Park. Named in her memory, the park offers dog wash areas and walkways, exercise equipment and a small lake.

The Copper Connection

While the slogan "Go West, Young Man" was still attracting newcomers to places like Arizona, and long before it was ever a state, the area was making history. Copper deposits were discovered, and companies like the Detroit Copper Mining Company in Morenci started to make money. Two New York men, Anson Phelps and William Dodge, invested in the company in 1881 and shortly thereafter formed a company of their own, Phelps Dodge. Freeport-McMoRan Copper & Gold Inc. acquired Phelps Dodge in March 2007, and today the company calls itself "one of the largest, most productive open-pit copper mining operations in the world."

Daring Feat

Edwin Eugene Aldrin, also known as "Buzz" by his friends, enjoyed a long, prestigious career as a pilot. He flew 66 missions during the Korean War, after which he returned to school and redirected his skyward energies to space travel. In 1963 he was among NASA's first picks to serve as astronaut, and on July 20, 1969, he became the second man to walk on the moon. In March 2007, Buzz added another notable experience to his lengthy résumé when he was one of the first people to walk the Grand Canyon's Skywalk—a glass-bottomed, horseshoe-shaped skywalk perched a full 4000 feet from its floor. Buzz has another solid connection to Arizona: he was married in Phoenix.

AMAZING ARIZONA The Grand Canyon's Skywalk is hailed as an engineering first. It cost $40 million and took more than one year to build. According to engineering tests conducted on the structure, it can "withstand the weight of 71 fully loaded Boeing 747 airplanes (more than 71 million pounds)...[and] winds in excess of 100 miles per hour from eight different directions."

CHECKING OUT THE FESTIVALS

First and Best

That Arizona is home to a number of rodeos isn't much of a surprise—it is cowboy country after all. But did you know the City of Prescott claims its rodeo is the oldest in the world? The story goes that the town's businessmen organized what they called at the time a "cowboy tournament" in 1888, and the event kicked off on July 4. Cash prizes were given to cowboys who proved their mettle in competitions like cattle roping, and the first to earn a professional, all-round title at that first-ever rodeo was Juan Leivas. The day was such a hit that Prescott started making plans for another rodeo the following year, and every year since 1888 their "World's Oldest" event just keeps getting bigger and better. The annual event runs for a full week, usually spanning into the first week of July, and along with the roping and riding, the Kiwanis Kiddie Parade, an arts and crafts show, rodeo queen contest, fun runs and a dance here and there make it a truly family-oriented experience.

Medieval Magic

Each of us, at one time or another, has wondered what it would have been like to live in a different era in history. Well, if you're in the vicinity of Apache Junction any time between early February and the end of March, you'll get the best opportunity ever to check out what life was like during one period of history—medieval England. The Arizona Renaissance Festival started out in 1989 and touts itself as being "one of the largest of the Renaissance events in the nation." Really, though, it's so much more than a festival. For almost two months visitors are treated to jousting tournaments, daylong feasts, ongoing period entertainment, an outdoor circus, and so much more, all in what really amounts to a Renaissance-themed fantasy village and amusement park rolled into one. The site covers 30 acres, includes 12 stages, 200 shops and more than 600 volunteers and workers dressed in period costumes. So be sure to check out this one-of-a-kind experience, where, in the words of the welcome opening at that first festival 20 years ago, "A king and his court, duelists, and ladies, crafts, food and games, an enchanted kingdom [are waiting] joust for you!"

Music in the Canyon

Serendipity is a wonderful thing. Without it we'd miss out so much in life. It was just such a happening that initiated the Grand Canyon Music Festival. As the story goes, Robert Bonfiglio and Clare Hoffman were hiking through the area in the early 1980s. As chance would have it, the head ranger of the day somehow knew the two were musicians and asked if they'd mind playing a tune or two for another ranger who was retiring. The pair agreed, set up a makeshift stage at the Cottonwood Campground and amidst that beautiful setting performed. They were such a hit that they were persuaded to establish a regular concert series, and in September 1984 the first Grand Canyon Music Festival was held. Today, the festival runs for three weeks in September "at the Shrine of Ages on the South Rim of Grand Canyon National Park." Bonfiglio and Hoffman are still involved—he as director and she as artistic director.

The Ostrich Festival

Chandler, Arizona, used to have ostrich ranches. Since 1989, it has had an annual Ostrich Festival. Held the second week of March and usually attended by around 300,000 people, the event is ranked as one of the "Top 10 Unique Festivals in the United States." Highlights include ostrich races and ostrich burgers.

The first ostriches in Arizona arrived in 1890, when Dr. J.N. Harbert brought a breeding pair to his farm at Alhambra, northwest of Phoenix. In those days, women's fashions demanded elaborate feathers, and soon ostrich ranches sprang up all over, with Arizona producing 80 percent of the ostrich plumes grown in the United States—only South Africa produced more.

DID YOU KNOW?

Arizona slang for ostrich is "longneck." Ostrich trivia: its scientific name, *Struthio camelus,* means "camel sparrow"; it is the world's fastest two-legged animal, able to run at 40 miles per hour; it lives 70 years; and each of its eyeballs (2 oz) is bigger than its brain (1.4 oz). And no, it doesn't taste like chicken—ostrich tastes like beef.

HAUNTINGS AND GHOST TOWNS

Flagstaff Pit Stop

It might be renowned as a roadhouse and dance club, but the "world famous" Museum Club in Flagstaff has more going for it than you might at first think. The club started out as a log house built in the 1930s by a taxidermist named Dean Eldredge. He had a vision of building the "biggest log cabin in the world" and housing his extensive collection of stuffed animals and other local artifacts. It may not have measured up to quite the monstrosity he'd imagined, but it was big. And the six-legged sheep and two-headed calves highlighting a collection of more than 30,000 items certainly attracted crowds.

During the five years Eldredge lived there, he operated his Museum Club as a museum, which acquired the nickname "The Zoo." Sadly, he died in 1936, most of his vast collection was sold off and the property turned over several times before a guitarist named Don Scott moved into the neighborhood and took over the business in 1963.

Scott had big visions, which included turning the roadhouse into a country music dance hall. Before long, big names like Willie Nelson and Barbara Mandrell started showing up and performing to an appreciative audience.

It was really Scott's efforts that put the Museum Club on the nightclub map, but his story is also filled with tragedy. One night in 1973, on her way to the couple's upstairs apartment, Don's wife Thorna slipped, fell and broke her neck. A few days later, she died. Heartbroken, Don attempted to continue on but two years later took his own life. Although the roadhouse has changed hands, been renovated and continues to be an evening hotspot, many visitors to the place believe it has a few more residents than most people think. Some have reported seeing Don and Thorna from time to time, and workers there have been known to report weird occurrences. So if you're traveling near Flagstaff, along Route 66, don't forget to take in this historic spot. You won't be disappointed.

Is Santa Dead?

On U.S. Highway 93, also between Chloride and Kingman, you might start asking yourself if you'd taken a wrong turn somewhere and ended up at the North Pole. Then again, if that's indeed the case, then kids the world over are in for a shock. What you've likely stumbled upon is the ruins of Santa Land. Back in the 1930s someone with a heart for Christmas and a good business sense developed a little village dedicated to Santa. Along with gift stores, and roadside grub, Santa Land offered its young visitors with an assortment of carnival rides.

Apparently the place was in business until 1995, but today all you can see are the remnants of a happier time and, maybe if you're lucky, the ghost of Christmas past.

DID YOU KNOW?

Arizona has 278 ghost towns. President Teddy Roosevelt and the King of Spain visited one of them, Adamana.

Welcome, One and All

Chloride isn't your ordinary, everyday kind of ghost town. Folks in this neck of the woods, both living and dead, routinely do everything they can to attract visitors. Chloride boasts a population of about 250 residents who, for the most part, make their living off of tourist traffic. Now, you may be wondering what's the big attraction in an almost ghost town like Chloride. Well, there are the Roy Purcell Murals for one. The well-known artist painted canyon walls surrounding Chloride with murals that tell stories of the area. Rock hounds and would-be gold diggers might be interested in the more than 70 abandoned mines surrounding the once-thriving community.

There are also tons of abandoned buildings, as there are with any ghost town, but in Chloride, if some of those buildings could talk, their stories would likely be x-rated—such as what remains of the "House of Soiled Doves," a former brothel. There's an assortment of abandoned mining equipment and tractors, gunfights are held on a regular basis throughout the summer months, and nature lovers can explore the flora and fauna, not to mention glimpse the wild mustangs thought to be descendants of the Spanish horses brought here by Spanish explorers. And along with all the ghostly rumblings you might discover in the local, ancient cemetery, you'll get plenty of living human contact too since many of the area residents are artists and sell their work at some of the finest stores in the county. Chloride is located on Mohave County Route 125, midway between Kingman, Arizona, and Boulder City, Nevada.

Some Famous Graves

- Country Music legend Waylon Jennings is buried at the Mesa City Cemetery.

- Doc Holliday's girlfriend, Big Nose Kate, died in Prescott in 1940 at the age of 90 and is buried there.

- The famous Mormon explorer Jacob Hamblin is buried at Alpine (Apache County).

- Gunfighter Johnny Ringo is buried in West Turkey Creek Canyon.

- Both Jacob Waltz, discoverer of the "Lost Dutchman Gold Mine," and Darrell Duppa, who named both Phoenix and Tempe, are buried in the Pioneer and Military Memorial Park in Phoenix.

- Walter Winchell is buried in Phoenix. He was the newspaper columnist who invented the gossip column. He had a national radio program that he always began with the memorable line, "Good Morning, Mr. and Mrs. North and South America and all the ships at sea: let's go to press!" From 1959 to 1963, he was the narrator for the popular television series *The Untouchables*.

- Barry Goldwater, 1964 presidential candidate, is buried in Paradise Valley.

- Erma Bombeck, the great columnist, is buried in Dayton, Ohio, her grave marked by a 29,000-pound Arizona boulder to commemorate the 25 happy years she and her husband lived in Paradise Valley.

The Man Who Was Buried in Three Places

Arizona's greatest mountain man was Pauline Weaver. His birth name was Powell, which Spanish speakers pronounced as *Powlin*. Known as "Prescott's First Citizen," he was born in Tennessee in 1797, and in October 1831 he became one of the first Americans ever to enter Arizona. A trapper and trader, he married a Native woman who may have been Maricopa or Pima. He died of malaria on June 21, 1867, and was buried in Camp Verde. But he didn't remain there. Fittingly for a man who had spent his life wandering, his body was disinterred in 1892 and transported to California and buried in San Francisco, and *then*, in 1929, he was dug up again and brought back to Arizona. This time he was buried in Prescott. More than 1000 people turned out to watch Boy Scouts carry his casket, followed by the Prescott High School Band. You can see Pauline Weaver's final gravesite today on the grounds of the Sharlot Hall Museum in downtown Prescott.

Biker Heaven?

Bellemont is another one of those communities that's listed as a sort-of ghost town with a handful of residents who welcome all visitors—especially the kind who ride big bikes like Harleys. Originally a water stop for steam-powered trains passing by, Bellemont was founded in 1882. The community was named after Belle Smith, daughter of a railroad superintendent, and by 1887 it had its own post office and sawmill. The town never really grew much, and during World War II it appeared to be the perfect place for the U.S. government to store and ship ammunition and explosives. By 1982, what became known as Camp Navajo was turned into a training facility by the Arizona National Guard.

Today, although most of the town's original buildings are in various stages of disrepair, Bellemont still attracts the odd ghost-town hopping visitor or two. Bikers making their way down Route 66 are also apt to stop by for a little grub at the Roadhouse Bar & Grill, or to check out the Grand Canyon Harley-Davidson dealership, and maybe even "crash" for the night in the nearby woods. And if you do visit the spot and get that eerie sense of déjà vu, don't fret. Chances are you have been there before if in no other way than through your television set while watching the movie *Easy Rider*, parts of which were filmed in the area.

The Devil's in the Name

With a name like Canyon Diablo (Devil's Canyon), it's no wonder this ghost town, located in Coconino County off the I-40, garnered an even more deadly reputation than the infamous towns of Tombstone and Dodge City. The town first came into existence in 1880, but it took some time to really set its foundation. This was partly because its growth depended on the completion of the railroad, which required a bridge to span either side of the canyon walls. Once that was completed, it was no-holds-barred, or so it seemed.

Because it didn't have any effective law enforcement, Canyon Diablo quickly earned a reputation as a wild place where lawlessness was the norm. To give you an idea of just how out of control this town was, when it finally got itself a sheriff, the man "pinned on a badge at 3:00 PM and was laid out for burial at 8:00 PM." At one point, worried townsfolk asked for the army's help in taming their rowdy community, but by then Canyon Diablo was already in decline.

If you're brave enough to tackle the terrain, and if you have a good set of wheels, several roads will take you up to what remains of the town. Once there you'll see remnants of several stone buildings, the grave of Herman Wolf—the only person believed to have died "peacefully" in the history of the town—and other assorted relics.

STRANGE STRUCTURES AND BIG THINGS

Look Up, Look Way Up!

Toddle along Cave Creek Road, just about six miles from the town of Carefree, and you'll come across what townsfolk call the "world's tallest kachina doll." Built in the 1950s by a sculptor from Scottsdale, Phillips Sanderson, and a Phoenix engineer, Carl Ludlow, the traditional Hopi Indian doll stretches 39 feet into the sky. It's a corn kachina, representing a plentiful harvest. Whereas most kachina dolls were carved in wood, this creation is solid concrete. A few years ago there was talk of its owner selling the kachina, but as of the writing of this book, the statue is still standing near Carefree, safe and sound.

The Fake Town

An entire Arizona town, seen by millions of people world-wide—on movie screens—is a fake town. Just west of Tucson, Old Tucson Studios is a Western town that was built solely for shooting movies. For the 1939 filming of *Arizona,* starring William Holden and Jean Arthur, more than 50 buildings were constructed in just 40 days. The "town" grew as more films were shot there, and in 1960 it was opened to the public. It's one of Southern Arizona's most popular attractions today.

Going to Congress—to See the Giant Frog

You can go to Congress to see the world's biggest frog. The desert area of Congress, in Arizona's Yavapai County, has quite a wide and varied history. Originally, the town was really two towns—"Mill Town" and "Lower Town." The area was mainly developed as a mining community in 1889, taking advantage of the gold boom of the day, and from its inception until the 1930s it boasted all the amenities of a thriving community. Since then, its population has dwindled, and Congress is really considered a ghost town. But in 1928, Sara Perkins, the wife of a newspaper-man named Eli, made a one-of-a-kind addition to the town that has lived on to this day. It appears Sara had quite the imagination, and on viewing a particularly large rock one day, saw in its form the outline of a frog. It was gray, of course, and needed a little creativity to enhance its features so everyone else would recognize what she saw. So she set out, with the help of her two young sons, to give it a little color.

The frog, now easily recognizable for anyone passing along the U.S. 89, put Congress on the map, so to speak. Travelers every-where knew of the "Congress Croaker," and many folks would come by just to check it out. Throughout the years, Sara touched up the frog's rich, green color and fine-tuned its black and white spots. In time, when it was no longer possible for an aging Sara to continue the demanding task, her sons took over.

And then when the last of the Perkins clan left the area, the townspeople took on the job—quite a feat when you consider the frog weighs 60 tons, stands about 16 feet tall and is surrounded by a barbed wire fence. If this wasn't all odd enough, it has a metal plaque that reads, "Jerry (Frog) Owens 1995." Apparently the man's ashes were scattered near the frog, but no one seems able to explain why.

Telling Time in a Big Way

In 1959, John Yellot (a solar engineer) and architect Joe Wong designed the Carefree Sundial. Located on Carefree Drive, this monstrosity, which points directly to the North Star, is 62 feet wide. At the time of its inception it was the largest sundial around, but today that title is being vied for by a number of communities worldwide. A sundial located in Lloydminster, Alberta, Canada, measures 197 feet wide and claims to be the world's largest. Many consider the "Samrat Yantra" in Jaipur, India, the largest sundial in the world (150 feet wide and 90 feet high). Either way, Carefree's "timepiece" is definitely a roadside attraction you should see.

TURBULENT TIMES

One Land, Many Owners

The man who defeated Davy Crockett at The Alamo later sold Tucson, Yuma, and the rest of Southern Arizona, to the United States for $10 million. Antonio López de Santa Anna, who had become the president of Mexico, got a good deal, because Mexico had owned the land for only 32 years. Before that, for 282 years, it belonged to Spain. And before that, for at least 4000 years, it belonged to the Akimel O'odham (Pima) and the Tohono O'odham (Papago) and their ancestors, the Hohokam.

DID YOU KNOW?

Arizona's most influential Italian, Eusebio Kino, was a Jesuit missionary who covered 50,000 miles on horseback. In 1699, Kino founded the Mission San Xavier del Bac, the "White Dove of the Desert" that you can visit today, about 10 miles south of downtown Tucson. Father Kino's hobby was carving wooden ships.

Soon Knocked Off the Front Page
To great media fanfare, Arizona became the 48th state and finally completed the American geographical puzzle—became the last contiguous state—on Valentine's Day in 1912, February 14. Sixty-one days later, the *Titanic* sank.

Civil War Roots
During the Civil War, exactly 20 days after he completed the Emancipation Proclamation that freed the slaves on January 1, 1863, President Abraham Lincoln freed Arizona from the Confederacy, signing the bill that created the Arizona Territory out of the New Mexico Territory. Confederate President Jefferson Davis was not pleased with either one of Lincoln's emancipation actions—two years earlier, Davis had created the Confederate Territory of Arizona.

Civil War's Westernmost Battle

Virtually the entire Civil War was fought east of the Mississippi. But both sides kept a wary eye on developments in the western territories, and on April 15, 1862, on the slopes of a volcanic spire called Picacho Pass, 50 miles northwest from Tucson, 13 Union soldiers and 10 Confederate soldiers accidentally bumped into each other, and shots were exchanged. In this, the Civil War's westernmost engagement (less a battle than a skirmish), all the losses were on the Union side: three killed and three wounded. Impossible to miss while driving on I-10 between Tucson and Phoenix, Picacho Pass with its 3374-foot volcanic spire is now a state park. *Picacho* is Spanish for "peak."

Daiquiri, Anyone?

When the American forces invaded Cuba at the start of the Spanish American War on June 22, 1898, they landed at the village of Daiquiri. To prepare for that war (in which 3289 Americans died), Teddy Roosevelt and his Rough Riders trained in Prescott, Arizona.

Arizona's Two Most Famous Dentists

Both of them studied dentistry in Pennsylvania, but each man gained lasting fame for his accomplishments in a different field in Arizona. After mastering the dental arts at the University of Pennsylvania, Zane Grey took up the literary arts, and his books almost single-handedly created the idealized image of the

Old West that today is accepted as the way things really were back then. That idealized image, "the Myth of the Old West," is why the *other* dentist remains so famous today: Doc Holliday.

John Henry Holliday earned a Doctor of Dental Surgery degree in Philadelphia, got tuberculosis, went west for the dry climate, got the nickname "Doc," and in Tombstone joined the Earps in the Gunfight at the O.K. Corral, October 26, 1881. Doc Holliday had a fearsome reputation but was usually drunk and kept missing the men he shot at. Having successfully killed only two men in gunfights during his lifetime, Doc died, of tuberculosis, at age 35.

Zane Grey, who was 15 when Doc Holliday died, passed away in 1939, age 67. His best-known novel, *Riders of the Purple Sage* (1912), created the Western genre in fiction (and in the movies), and two of his other novels inspired the greatest Old West heroes of both the United States and Canada: his *Lone Star Ranger* (1915) inspired the Lone Ranger (and his faithful stallion, Silver), and his *King of the Royal Mounted* (1936) inspired both RCMP Sergeants Dave King and William Preston (and his lead sled dog, Yukon King).

A Zane Grey fishing story inspired Ernest Hemingway to write *The Old Man and the Sea*. Among the 130 movies based on Zane Grey novels were the films that launched the careers of Tom Mix, Randolph Scott, Shirley Temple and John Wayne. Grey wrote 57 novels, 10 nonfiction Westerns, 200 short stories and scores of hunting and fishing articles and books. One of the first authors ever to become a millionaire, Grey referred to the state as "My beloved Arizona," and many of his best-loved books were written in his cabin on the Mogollon Rim. The cabin burned down in the Dude Fire of 1990, but an exact replica opened in 2005 and is open to visitors today near the Rim Country Museum at Green Valley Park in Payson (Gila County).

DID YOU KNOW?

Zane was his middle name. At birth he was given the name
Pearl Zane Gray, and later in life he dropped his first name and
changed the spelling of his last name to Grey.

The USS *Arizona*—All Three of Them

In 1819, the U.S. Congress established the protocol that first-
class ships would be named after states, second-class ships after
rivers and third-class ships after cities and towns. There have
been three warships, not just one, called USS *Arizona*. The first,
launched in 1859, was an iron-hulled side-wheel steamer that
saw action in the Civil War. The second, launched in 1865, was
a wooden frigate with two massive engines. The third and more
famous battleship USS *Arizona*, sunk at Pearl Harbor, was built
in Brooklyn. It was christened on June 19, 1915, by Arizona pioneer Ester Ross of Prescott, first with a bottle of champagne and
then with a bottle of the first water to pass over the spillway of
Roosevelt Dam. This *Arizona* was 608 feet long and 106 feet at
its widest, displaced 37,654 tons and had a draft of 33 feet
6 inches. Its rudder measured 443 square feet; its main guns
were 52 feet long; and it could fire 1400-pound projectiles
19.32 miles. The Pearl Harbor Memorial in Hawaii is positioned above the *Arizona,* in which 1177 men perished on
December 7, 1941. You can see one of its two 20,000-pound
anchors today at Pearl Harbor; the other one is in front of the
State Capitol in Phoenix.

Hitler's Arizona Connection

From his childhood and throughout his adult life, Adolph
Hitler's favorite author was Karl May. One of the best-selling
German authors of all time (more than 200 million copies of his
books have been sold), May wrote 16 novels set in Arizona, New
Mexico and Texas, the first one appearing in 1879. Each novel

recounted an adventure by the German superman hero, Old Shatterhand, and his faithful companion, an Apache named Winnetou. Encountering disrespect from "inferior" tribes, the two friends exterminated everyone. Late in World War II, although the Third Reich was running out of money for bullets, Hitler ordered a massive reprinting of his favorite May novel so that each soldier on the Eastern Front could have his own personal copy. According to Klaus Mann (*The Kenyon Review*, Autumn 1940), "The Third Reich is Karl May's ultimate triumph, the ghastly realization of his dreams. It is according to ethical and aesthetic standards indistinguishable from his that the Austrian house-painter, nourished in his youth by Old Shatterhand, is now attempting to rebuild the world." And what about the swastika? Well, it appeared on the cover of many of May's "Arizona novels," identified as an ancient Apache symbol.

SKELETONS IN ARIZONA'S CLOSET

The Indian School

Indian School Road takes its name from the Phoenix Indian School that was located at 24th Street. At the school's opening in September 1891, Indian Commissioner Thomas Morgan said, "It's cheaper to educate Indians than to kill them." From then until 1935, the school's "assimilation" policy meant trying to force the Indian children to stop being Indian.

The Japanese Internment Camps

On February 19, 1942, President Franklin Delano Roosevelt signed the order creating camps where Americans of Japanese ancestry were to be imprisoned. Of the 10 camps built, two were in Arizona, including the biggest one of them all, the Poston Relocation Camp (Yuma County), which held 17,814 prisoners. The other one, the Gila River Relocation Camp (Maricopa County), held 13,348 men, women and children who were guilty of the "crime" of being Asian.

The Thanksgiving Day Riot

On Thanksgiving night in 1942, an off-duty African American soldier who had been drinking heavily got into an argument with an African American woman and hit her with a beer bottle. When the soldier brandished a knife at the officer attempting to arrest him, the officer shot and wounded him. Seeing this, other African American soldiers protested, whereupon the order went out to round up 150 African American soldiers at random and transport them to the nearby Papago Park Military Installation, where Nazi POWs were being held. African American troops then scattered into Phoenix neighborhoods that were predominately African American. To "flush them out," armored personnel carriers rolled into a cordoned-off area of 28 blocks and started firing 50-caliber machine guns into civilian homes, each bullet making a fist-size hole. The evening ended with three men killed, 11 wounded and 180 arrested and jailed.

The Long Walk

Beginning in the freezing days of January 1863, the army forced the Navajo to walk from their ancestral homeland in northeast Arizona to Bosque Redondo, in southeastern New Mexico. More than 200 men, women and children died. Within two years, 9022 Navajo and Mescalero Apaches were interned there. The man in charge of the Long Walk was Colonel Christopher "Kit" Carson, who instituted a "scorched-earth" policy in the Navajo homeland, burning homes, crops and trees and killing livestock, to force the Navajo to leave.

The Bisbee Deportations

Following a 1917 strike, 1186 striking miners were loaded aboard boxcars that were inches deep in manure. Guarded by 186 deputies and a machine gun mounted on the top of the train, the men were taken east and abandoned at Hermanas, New Mexico.

The Oatman Massacre

In central Arizona on February 18, 1851, a man, his pregnant wife and three of their children were murdered by Native Americans later said to be Yavapai-Apache. Another son, left for dead, survived, and two daughters, 13-year-old Olive and seven-year-old Mary Ann, were taken into captivity. Tortured and held as slaves, the girls were eventually traded to Mohave Indians for a few horses and taken to a camp near Needles, California, where they were again tortured. Mary Ann died there, and after two years with the Mohave, Olive was traded to the military outpost at Yuma for some trade goods. A book about Olive's ordeal, by Royal B. Stratton, became an antebellum bestseller, selling 30,000 copies. The town of Oatman (Mohave County) was named in honor of Olive, who died in 1903 at age 65.

DID YOU KNOW?

Hollywood greats Clark Gable and Carole Lombard honeymooned in Oatman in 1939, after being married in Kingman.

Proyecto de Guerra (**"Project for War"**)
In 1835, the year before the Battle of the Alamo, the Mexican state of Sonora, immediately to the south of Arizona, put a bounty on Apaches: 100 pesos for a man's scalp, 50 for a woman's and 25 for a child's. One peso was equivalent to one dollar. This genocide program was called off after it was learned that trappers and mountain men were slaughtering peaceful Arizona Indians (Pima, Papago) for their scalps.

The Camp Grant Massacre

At dawn on April 30, 1871, a mob of angry Tucson citizens descended upon nearby Camp Grant and clubbed, shot, raped and mutilated 144 Aravaipa Apache people, mostly women and children. Upon learning of this, President Ulysses S. Grant threatened to put the entire Arizona Territory under martial law unless those who had committed the atrocity were brought to justice. More than 100 defendants were eventually tried, and the jury took 19 minutes to acquit them.

The Skeleton Canyon Massacre

In July 1881, Mexican bandits known as the Estrada Gang looted the town of Monterrey, Mexico. Escaping into Arizona through Skeleton Canyon, 40 miles east of Tombstone, the gang had 30 mules packed with $75,000 worth of coins, jewels and artifacts. When the Mexican bandits stopped for the night in a place called Devil's Kitchen, a gang of American bandits ambushed them, killing 19 men.

The Pleasant Valley War

Two Arizona families, the cattle-herding Grahams and the sheep-raising Tewksburys, battled over grazing rights and virtually annihilated each other in America's most violent blood feud. Over the course of 10 years, the feud claimed 20 lives. The Pleasant Valley War finally ended in 1892, when the last Graham was gunned down in the street during a visit to Tempe. The town of Pleasant Valley subsequently changed its name to Young. Today you can tour the battle sites and see a few still-standing bullet-riddled log cabins, and watch the annual Pleasant Valley Days parade (third weekend in July).

The Short Creek Raid

On July 26, 1953, at Short Creek (Mohave County), an incident occurred that the media at the time called "the largest mass arrest of men and women in modern American history." A force of Arizona State Police and U.S. National Guardsmen swooped into the polygamous community and arrested the entire population of 400 people—then released the seven people who turned out not to be Mormon fundamentalists. Among those arrested were 236 children, and 150 of them were not reunited with their parents until two years later.

BE IT EVER SO HUMBLE

Wikiups and Hogans

The Native American, domed, single-room dwelling made of branches and thatch that back East is called a *wigwam,* is called, in Arizona, a *wikiup.* The various Apache tribes built wikiups. The Navajo version of the wikiup is the *hogan.* A *kiva* is a sacred room constructed of adobe by Pueblo tribes for religious ceremonies. The *tipi* was never used by Arizona tribes.

America's Oldest Continuous Community

When Richard the Lionheart of England, born in 1157, was still a little boy, the town of Oraibi was founded in Arizona. That was more than a century before the Apache and the Navajo migrated south from Canada. On Third Mesa of the Hopi Reservation, near Kykotsmovi, Oraibi is the oldest continuously inhabited community in the U.S.—now close to nine centuries old. Compared to "Old Oraibi," Arizona towns like Tubac, established in 1752 when George Washington was 20 years old, seem fairly recent—and towns such as Scottsdale, incorporated in 1951, seem brand new. By 1890, about 905—or half the Hopi population of Arizona—called Oraibi home. Today it's no longer the cultural center for the Hopi people that it once was, but people still live there. In 1964, Oraibi was declared a National Historic Landmark and is also listed on the National Register of Historic Places.

Towns Where Time Stands Still

Three time-banned towns, where their history is their present identity and their future, are Tombstone, Prescott and Jerome. To go to Tombstone is to step back into the 1880s; to go to Prescott is to glimpse Territorial Arizona; and to go to Jerome is to see Arizona's wild mining days.

America's Biggest Future City

The biggest city in the United States might one day be in Arizona: for more than 50 years, people have been predicting that Phoenix and Tucson, 120 miles apart, will expand until they merge into a single gigantic megalopolis.

The Nine Types of Arizona Community

Arizona has nine different types of community: mega-city, suburban city, city, town, village, camp, ghost town, time-banned town and imaginary place. It was an imaginary place that first brought conquistadors into Arizona in the mid-1500s, the Seven Cities of Cibola, where people were said to eat on gold plates. An imaginary place that was actually built is the "experimental town" of Arcosanti. The dream-come-true community of architect Paolo Soleri, Arcosanti was founded in 1970 about 70 miles north of Phoenix.

Tiny Places

Arizona has scores of camps or communes where a small number of people enjoy the opposite of big-city life. The most famous is Tortilla Flat, with a population of five. It's located in the Superstition Mountains, east of Phoenix.

Not Quite Cities

Of villages and towns—defined as having more than 1000 residents but fewer than 6000—there are 456 in Arizona, including:

Carefree (2927)	Kayenta (4922)
Cave Creek (3728)	Litchfield Park (3810)
Claypool (1794)	Munds Park (1250)
Chinle (5366)	Oracle (3563)
Dolan Springs (1867)	Pinetop-Lakeside (3582)
Dudleyville (1323)	Queen Creek (4316)
Eagar (4033)	Rio Verde (1419)
Fort Defiance (4061)	Springerville (1972)
Gila Bend (1980)	Sweetwater (5657)
Grand Canyon Village (1460)	Village of Oak Creek (5245)
Heber-Overgaard (2722)	Wickenburg (5082)
Holbrook (4917)	Wilcox (3733)
Huachuca City (5295)	Williams (2842)
Kachina Village (2664)	Window Rock (3059)

True Cities

Including Prescott, which with 33,938 residents is both a time-banned town and a real city, Arizona has 81 cities (6000 or more people) including:

Apache Junction (31,814)

Bisbee (6090)

Bullhead City (33,769)

Camp Verde (9451)

El Mirage (7609)

Flagstaff (52,894)

Florence (17,054)

Gilbert (109,697)

Glendale (218,812)

Kingman (20,069)

Lake Havasu City (41,938)

Marana (13,556)

Oro Valley (29,700)

Page (6809)

Paradise Valley (13,664)

Payson (13,620)

Peoria (108,364)

Phoenix (1,505,265)

Scottsdale (202,705)

Sedona (10,192)

Tempe (158,625)

Tuba City (8225)

Tucson (486,699)

Winslow (9520)

Yuma (77,515)

Scottsdale

Although it has a "small-town" feel, the city of Scottsdale is *big*—it's 184.4 square miles. In comparison, Manhattan is 22.7 square miles, Miami, Florida, is 35.68 square miles, and Boston is 89.6 square miles.

☞ Current or former Scottsdale residents include TV announcer and host Hugh Downs (a direct descendant of Davy Crockett), and Elisabeth Kubler-Ross, author of *Death and Dying* (1969), who *Time* magazine in 1999 called one of the "100 Most Important Thinkers" of the 20th century.

☞ Baseball immortal Ted Williams also still lives in Scottsdale—maybe. Considered the greatest hitter ever to play the game, Williams died in 2002 and was put into cryogenic suspension at a facility in Scottsdale, the Alcor Life Extension Foundation.

Paradise Valley

So named in 1899 because of its abundance of wildflowers, Paradise Valley today has an abundance of wealthy people: in 2006, the median price for a house there was $1.74 million. Current or former Paradise Valley residents include boxer Mike Tyson; Jessie Owens, the athlete who irritated Hitler by beating all the Aryans at the 1936 Olympics in Berlin; Leona Helmsley, owner of the Empire State Building; cartoonist Bill Keane (creator in 1961 of *Family Circus,* which is still being syndicated); and former Vice President Dan Quayle.

Mesa

The largest suburban city in America and the second largest on the continent— only Mississauga, Ontario, is bigger—is Mesa, Arizona. With 460,155 people (in 2006), Mesa is bigger than St. Louis, Minneapolis or Cleveland.

The Capital

Population-wise, Phoenix with more than 1.5 million people is the largest of America's 50 state capitals, as well as the country's fifth-largest city—only New York, Los Angeles, Chicago and Houston have more people. Slightly larger than Los Angeles (498.3 square miles), Phoenix (517.17 square miles) is also the county seat of Maricopa County.

PetSmart, with more than 1000 retail stores throughout the U.S. and Canada, is headquartered in Phoenix. So is CSK Auto, one of the largest retailers of automotive parts and accessories in America. Also headquartered in Phoenix: Freeport-McMoRan, one of the world's largest producers of gold and copper; U-Haul International, which has 18,000 employees; Allied Waste Industries, the second-largest waste management company in the U.S.; and Avnet, the world's largest franchised distributor of electronic components and subsystems.

DID YOU KNOW?

The first McDonald's franchise in the world opened in Phoenix in 1953.

Famous Phoenicians

Current or former Phoenix residents include Harry Cohn, co-founder of Columbia Pictures; World War II cartoonist Bill Mauldin, creator of the character G.I. Joe; and singer Rod Stewart. Amanda Blake, who for 19 years played Kitty on the TV show *Gunsmoke,* lived in Phoenix with her own 11 full-grown "kitties": 10 cheetahs and an African lion.

Before the Zoo was a Zoo...

The Phoenix Zoo of today had different cages during World War II: it was a camp for German and Italian POWs.

The Old Pueblo

☞ Tucson, long nicknamed "the Old Pueblo," is the site each February for the largest gem and mineral show in the world—the Tucson Gem and Mineral show regularly attracts 50,000 people from more than 20 countries. Also in Tucson each February is the *Fiesta de los Vaqueros,* or Rodeo Week, which also boasts "the world's largest non-mechanized parade."

☞ Tucson has belonged to three different countries: Spain, Mexico and the United States—and to three different versions of the United States:

1775—Spain established a presidio, or fort, in Tucson

1821—With Mexican independence, Tucson became part of Mexico

1853—Mexico sold Tucson to the United States (Gadsden Purchase)

1861–62—Tucson was the capital of the Confederate Arizona Territory

1863—Tucson (and all of Arizona) was part of the New Mexico Territory

1867–79—Tucson was the capital of the Arizona Territory

☞ Large numbers of Chinese people came to Tucson with the railroad in 1880. Most came from the Kwangtung districts of Toy San, Sum Yip and San Wai. Many stayed to set up small farms along the Santa Cruz River.

☞ Current or former residents of Tucson include actors Lee Marvin and Stephen Baldwin; environmentalist Edward Abbey; mobster Joe Bonanno; astronaut Frank Borman; author Ray Bradbury; producer Jerry Bruckheimer (*Beverly Hills Cop, Pirates of the Caribbean*); TV entertainer Geraldo

Rivera; painter Ted DeGrazia; chimpanzee researcher Jane Goodall; Lalo Guerrero, "Father of Chicano Music"; and singers John Denver, Linda Ronstadt and Paul McCartney.

Jojo's Home

When Paul and Linda McCartney lived in Tucson, a popular bar at the time was called Jojo's. Both the bar and the city were immortalized in the song "Get Back." The Beatles' first U.S. single, released in 1969, the song tells the tale of Jojo, who left his home in Tucson, Arizona.

Some Arizona Place Names

☛ Eloy (Pinal County) comes from "My God!" in Syrian: *Eloi!*

☛ Mammoth (Pinal County) was named not for the woolly mammoths that once roamed there but for its mammoth ore deposits.

☛ Buckeye (Maricopa County) was named for Ohio.

☛ Miami (Gila County) was named for Miami, Ohio.

☛ Coolidge (Pinal County) was named for President Calvin Coolidge, and Hoover Dam, on the Arizona-Nevada border, was named for President Herbert Hoover.

☛ Jerome (Yavapai County) was named after New York attorney Eugene Jerome.

☛ Ehrenberg (La Paz County) was named for German engineer Herman Ehrenberg, and Wickenburg (Maricopa County) was named for Austrian Heinrich Wickenburg.

☛ Douglas (Cochise County) was named for Canadian doctor Stewart Douglas (born in Quebec in 1868).

☛ Fountain Hills (Maricopa County) was named for its fountain, which for 10 years after it was built in 1971 was the tallest fountain in the world (560 feet).

☛ Florence (Pinal County) was named by its founder, Levi Ruggles, for two of his three daughters, Flora and Florence (but not for Cynthia).

☛ Sedona (Coconino County) was named by Ellsworth Schnebly for his sister-in-law, Sedona Schnebly.

☛ Salome (La Paz County) was named by Charles H. Pratt not for Salome, the biblical temptress, but for his own wife Grace, whose middle name was Salome.

☛ Show Low (Navajo County) was named for a card game called Seven-Up. Corydon E. Cooley and Marion Clark agreed that, "Whoever shows low gets to name the town." Clark's cards went over, at which time Cooley threw down his winning hand and said, "Show Low it is."

☛ Surprise (Maricopa County) was so named because everyone was surprised it came into existence.

☛ Hope (La Paz County) was so named because everyone hoped it would grow.

☛ Why (Pima County) got its name thanks to a bureaucratic rule. People there wanted to call their community simply "Y," because State Routes 85 and 86 made a Y-shaped intersection nearby—but Arizona law required all city names to have a minimum of three letters.

☛ Everyone today is relieved that an Englishman named Darrell Duppa suggested that Hayden's Ferry should change its name to Tempe, and that Pumpkinville should change its name to Phoenix.

The Big House

Built by the Hohokam people around 1350 AD, Casa Grande (Spanish for "big house)" is one of the largest prehistoric structures ever built in North America. Four stories tall, it was the first cultural and prehistoric site ever to be protected by the United States government. President Benjamin Harrison made it the nation's first archeological reserve in 1892, and President Woodrow Wilson made it a National Monument in 1918. Casa Grande (population 34,554) is named after the ruins, which are actually in Coolidge (7786 people).

Community Trivia

☛ Alpine is at an elevation of 8050 feet in Apache County. In 1880 the settlers built a log-house fort about one mile southeast of the present Alpine. Bush Valley is said to be the highest place in United States where farming is successful.

☛ Guadalupe is a Yaqui Indian village that lies immediately south of Tempe. It's named in honor of *Nuestra Señora de Guadalupe,* the especially Mexican manifestation of the Virgin Mary.

☛ Fredonia and Colorado City are in the "Arizona Strip"—the part of the state north of the Grand Canyon.

☛ Somerton, 12 miles south of Yuma and equidistant from the California and Mexico borders, is located at an elevation of 103 feet.

☛ Chandler was founded in 1912 by Alexander John Chandler, who was from Coaticock, Quebec. He had been appointed the first veterinary surgeon for the Territory of Arizona, arriving in August 1887. A friend of Frank Lloyd Wright, Chandler died in 1950.

☛ Yuma used to be called Arizona City. The name lives on in Arizona City, established in Pinal County in 1962. Mohave County has Arizona Village.

☛ Current or former residents Flagstaff include singer Glen Campbell, cowboy actor Andy Devine, and Clyde Tombaugh, who discovered Pluto.

☛ Current or former residents of Sedona include Hollywood stars Al Pacino, Sean Young, Lucille Ball, Jane Russell, Debbie Reynolds, Orson Welles and Ted Danson.

☛ Arizona's "Tri-City area" is composed of Prescott and the towns of Prescott Valley (seven miles east) and Chino Valley (16 miles north). The population of the Tri-City area in 2007 was 122,000.

☛ Prescott was named after a blind Massachusetts historian, William H. Prescott, whose most famous book, *The Conquest of Mexico,* was published in 1843. The town was the Territorial capital twice, from 1863 to 1867, and from 1877 to 1889—the capital was moved to Tucson in 1867, and to Phoenix in 1889.

☛ Virgil Earp and his wife Allie lived in Prescott, where Virgil owned a sawmill at Thumb Butte and was town constable. His brothers Wyatt and Morgan visited him in Prescott before they left for Tombstone, and Virgil joined them in Tombstone eight months later.

The Biltmore

Contrary to popular belief, the luxurious Arizona Biltmore Hotel was not designed by Frank Lloyd Wright, but by Albert Chase McArthur, who was Wright's apprentice. The Biltmore opened in Phoenix at the end of the Roaring Twenties (1929), and it remains one of the city's most famous and exclusive resorts. Actor Nicholas Cage honeymooned there with his former wife Patricia Arquette, and again later with new wife Lisa Marie Presley. But the Biltmore is more famous for this fact: every U.S. President since Herbert Hoover has stayed there.

Creative Disasters

Various natural disasters helped to form many of Arizona's communities. South Phoenix has been impoverished since the Salt River's great flood in 1891, when the water reached Washington Street—after that, all the Anglos moved to North Phoenix. Phoenix is named for the mythic bird that rose from the ashes of its own funeral pyre, but Bullhead City did that literally, after its total destruction by fire in 1873.

The same happened to downtown Prescott in "the Great Fire of 1900." For four hours on the night of July 14, fire swept through Whiskey Row and downtown Prescott. More than 80 businesses burned to the ground, but no one died or was injured, and Prescott reemerged from the ashes a more beautiful city. In The Palace Saloon and Restaurant today, you can see the ornately carved 1880s Brunswick bar that patrons carried to safety across the street to the plaza that night.

DID YOU KNOW?

The word "Yuma" comes from the Old Spanish word *umo,* "smoke." The Native people in Yuma used to make enormous bonfires to induce rain, creating tremendous clouds of smoke.

Worst Wildfire

The largest and most devastating wildfire in Arizona history was the Rodeo-Chediski fire that burned 467,066 acres (more than twice the size of Mesa, Chandler, Tempe and Scottsdale combined) between Heber and Show Low from June 18 to July 7, 2002. Some 30,000 people had to be evacuated, 426 structures were lost, and the suppression cost was $153 million. The conflagration began as two separate fires that merged into one. The first was started by an unemployed firefighter trying to generate work for himself; the other was started by a lost hiker lighting a signal flare to get the attention of a news helicopter. The arsonist was sentenced to 10 years; the hiker was not charged.

Worst Aviation Disaster

On June 30, 1956, Arizona's worst aviation disaster took place about an hour after two airplanes took off from Los Angeles International Airport just three minutes apart from one another. The United Airlines DC-7, with 58 people aboard, was headed to Chicago, and the TWA Super Constellation, with 70 people, was headed to Kansas City, Missouri. Above the Grand Canyon, they collided. All 128 people died. The wreckage was strewn around the area where the Colorado River and the Little Colorado join. Professional mountain rescue teams were flown in from Switzerland to help recover the bodies. This accident led to dramatic improvements in the U.S. air traffic control system.

STRANGELY KIND LIVING

"I love Arizona. People are really strange and kind."

–Sharon Stone, actress

Lifestyles Aplenty

There is no one "Arizona lifestyle." Here people find everything from fast and frenzied big-city life to slower and saner small-town life, and from urban to rural, and from totally climate-controlled to totally in touch and in tune with nature.

Perceived Class System

There is no class system in Arizona—officially. Having made an industry of elegance in everything from condominiums to cuisine, Scottsdale is sometimes playfully called "Snobsdale." Tusconians look down their noses at Phoenicians, and Sedonites pity everyone else for not having cool vortexes. The people of Flagstaff, Payson and Prescott try not to show their superiority over all lowlanders. Those who herd cattle, tend sheep, and hunt or fish, and those who want to protect animals and fish from hunters and fishermen, all try to tolerate each other. And real cowboys try not to laugh at people who just dress like cowboys.

"Cowpeople"

"Cowboy" used to be a nasty name in Arizona, synonymous with outlaw, cattle rustler, thief and murderer. In the Gunfight at the O.K. Corral, the Earps and Doc were blazing away at members of a gang who called themselves the Cowboys. Once those wild times were more or less tamed, the term and its female counterpart came to stand for the opposite: honorable, rugged, independent men and women who worked cattle on horseback.

At Western stores throughout Arizona, the best-selling items are cowboy hats, shirts and boots, especially to tourists. But it isn't the outfit that makes a cowboy, or a cowgirl, it's the mindset. Dale Evans (who wrote the song "Happy Trails," and was the wife of Roy Rogers on-screen and off) said it best: "There's more to being a cowgirl than punching cows, or winning rodeo trophies, or galloping off into a movie sunset with Roy. Cowgirl is an attitude, really. A pioneer spirit, a special American brand of courage. The cowgirl faces life head on, lives by her own lights, and makes no excuses. Cowgirls take stands. They speak up. They defend the things they hold dear. A cowgirl might be a rancher, or a barrel racer, or a bull rider, or an actress. But she's just as likely to be a checker at the local Winn Dixie, a full-time mother, a banker, an attorney, an astronaut." Or, Evans might have added, a Supreme Court justice—Sandra Day O'Connor is in the National Cowgirl Hall of Fame in Fort Worth, Texas.

Religious Freedom

There were those who came to Arizona for the same reason the Pilgrims came to America: for a lifestyle free from religious persecution. In the northern part of the state (Coconino County), Mormon settlers literally named their new town for "freedom from federal law," Fredonia. But the law, opposed to the polygamous lifestyle, eventually intruded. In 1957 State of Arizona officials swept into Millennial City (Mohave County) on a polygamy raid and rounded up 200 women and children. The state eventually let them all go as its case fizzled, but the publicity was so negative that in 1958 the town changed its name to Colorado City. In January 2004, Warren Jeffs, absolute ruler of the Fundamentalist Church of Jesus Christ of Latter-day Saints, expelled a group of 20 men from Colorado City, including the mayor, and reassigned their wives and children to other men. Jeffs, now in prison, was said to have 70 wives.

DID YOU KNOW?

Chiricahua Apache shaman and war leader Geronimo had nine wives, at times three simultaneously.

Freedom from Kids

Most Arizona cities welcome families, but if you don't particularly want to be around rug-rats, then we have whole communities where children are not allowed to live, including:

Academy Village (Tucson)

Canoa Ranch (Green Valley)

Castlerock Village (Kingman)

Encanterra (Queen Creek)

Fulton Ranch (Chandler)

Hassayampa Village (Prescott)

Las Campanas (Green Valley)

Mission Royale (Casa Grande)

Ocotillo (Chandler)

Prescott Lakes (Prescott)

Saddlebrooke Ranch (Oracle)

Seville Golf & Country Club (Chandler)

Springfield (Chandler)

Sunbird (Chandler)

Sundance (Buckeye)

Victorian Estates (Prescott)

The Villages at Lynx Creek (Prescott Valley)

Westbrook Village (Peoria)

Freedom from…Poverty!

But far more plentiful than those seeking freedom from religious persecution have been those who came to Arizona for the same reason people flocked to California in 1849 and to the Yukon in 1897: freedom from poverty, the chance of sudden wealth. In numerous Arizona stampedes, just like in the California Gold Rush and the Klondike Gold Rush, religion was the *last* thing on people's minds. In 1903 a New York newspaper called Jerome "the wickedest town in the West." Wicked towns being a thing of the past, today's "gold-rushers" don't trek off into Arizona's hills to find freedom from poverty—they trek to all the casinos.

Casinos

Casinos owned and operated by Arizona's Native American tribes and nations generate a great deal of money: $1.94 billion in 2007. The slot machines at the two Casino Arizona casinos in Scottsdale are said to pay out $7.1 million every day. Here are the state's 26 most popular Native American casinos:

Apache Gold Casino (San Carlos)

Bluewater Resort & Casino (Parker)

Bucky's & Yavapai Casinos (Prescott)

Bucky's Casino (Prescott)

Casino Arizona at Indian Bend (Scottsdale)

Casino Arizona at McKellips (Scottsdale)

Casino del Sol (Tucson)

Casino of the Sun (Tucson)

Cliff Castle Casino (Camp Verde)

Cocopah Bingo & Casino (Somerton)

Desert Diamond Casino Pima Mine Road (Tucson)

Desert Diamond Casino (Tucson)

Fort McDowell Casino (Fountain Hills)

Gila River Casino at Lone Butte (Chandler)

Gila River Casino at Vee Quiva (Laveen)

Gila River Casino at Wild Horse Pass (Chandler)

Golden Ha:Sañ Casino (the town of Why, 30 miles from the Mexican border)

Harrah's Ak-Chin Casino Resort (the town of Maricopa)

Hon-Dah Resort Casino (Pinetop)

Lehi Community Building (Mesa)

Lone Butte Casino (Chandler)

Mazatzal Hotel & Casino (Payson)

Quechan Paradise Casino Arizona (Yuma)

Salt River Community Building (Scottsdale)

Spirit Mountain Casino (Mohave Valley)

Yavapai Bingo (Prescott)

Freedom from Thirst

After a hard day of hunting for gold or herding cattle, early Arizonans said, in effect, "It's time to go get drunk!" From their powerful thirst came saloons and Arizona's nightlife, which used to be pretty wild. In 1882, the *New York Times* called Tombstone's Bird Cage Opera House Saloon "the roughest, bawdiest, and most wicked night spot between Basin Street and the Barbary Coast." For nine years the Bird Cage never closed its doors, operating 24 hours a day. During those years, 16 gunfights and knife fights took 26 lives on the premises. There are still 140 bullet holes throughout the building, marking the ceilings, walls, and floors. The Bird Cage, now a museum, is one of modern Tombstone's most popular attractions.

DID YOU KNOW?

Today the United States ranks 40th in the world in alcohol consumption, and Arizona ranks 16th in America, with 28 gallons consumed per person per year.

The Long Reign of The Palace

Arizona's greatest saloon from those days was—and still is—in Prescott: The Palace. It is currently the oldest saloon and restaurant in Arizona (try the Rough Riders Ribeye or, in honor of silent-movie cowboy star Tom Mix, the Tom Mixed Grill—sirloin, citrus salmon and shrimp scampi). The Palace opened on South Montezuma Street in September 1877. Soon there were 26 other saloons on that same block, which then was called Whiskey Row. Some of the saloons brewed their own beer. A glass of beer cost 5¢, and most of the hard drinks cost 12½¢ each. Men frequently paid for their drinks—and female companionship—with gold dust.

The Palace was much more than just a saloon. It had three large gaming tables for faro, poker, roulette, keno and craps, and it also had a Chinese restaurant, a barbershop and a theater for celebrities. A Syrian woman named Farida Mazar Spyropoulos and nicknamed "Little Egypt" shocked and delighted America with her erotic dancing at the World's Columbian Exposition in Chicago in 1893. Her "Hoochee-Coochee" dance also delighted, but probably didn't shock, the residents of Prescott when she danced at The Palace in 1910.

Firewater

Contrary to popular belief, the white man did not introduce Native Americans to alcohol—they introduced *easier* alcohol: store-bought firewater. For centuries the Papago (Tohono O'odham) people had fermented saguaro fruit to make a wine that was said to be far more intoxicating than whiskey, and the Pima Indians made their own traditional wine, called *tesquino,* from fermented corn.

Dry in Frisco

San Francisco, "Frisco," was famous for its Barbary Coast, where sin was big business. Arizona's Frisco, in Mohave County, however, was famous for being the only mining town with no saloon—the reason being, people said, that most of the miners there were married and their wives wanted them to stay sober and out of trouble. There may be a moral in the fact that Frisco is a ghost town today.

All Things Naughty

During Territorial times, prostitution was common and only marginally regulated. In Tombstone, everyone knew that the "bird cages" at the Bird Cage Opera House Saloon were private boxes upstairs where prostitutes plied their trade for $25 a night. Today, of course, prostitution is *totally* against the law in Arizona (wink wink), and women are *never* viewed as mere sexual objects.

DID YOU  KNOW?

Porn star Raven Riley, born in 1986, lives in Arizona. And in 2005, porn star Jenna Jameson purchased Babe's, a strip club in Scottsdale.

Playboy Playmates Born in Arizona

Miss February 1957: Sally Todd, Tucson

Miss November 1963: Terre Tucker, Arizona

Miss August 1965: Lannie Balcom, Clarkdale

Miss January 1973: Miki Garcia, Kingman

Miss September 1973: Geri Glass, Phoenix

Miss September 1975: Mesina Miller, Arizona

Miss April 1983: Christina Ferguson, Phoenix

Miss March 1991: Julie Clarke, Tucson

Miss March 1999: Alexandria Karlsen, Mesa

Miss April 2001: Katie Lohmann, Scottsdale

Charges Dropped After Bra Dropped

Canadian sex symbol Pamela Anderson (born in Ladysmith, British Columbia), who appeared on the cover of *Playboy* magazine 10 times, was almost jailed in Arizona. During a *Playboy* photo shoot on historic Route 66 in 1992, she was arrested for indecent exposure, read her rights and taken to the police station. She argued that she was not guilty of the charge since "only one nipple was sticking out" of her sheer dress. To have the charge dropped, Anderson agreed to write a letter of apology to the Baptist minister who happened to live a few hundred yards from the shoot location.

DID YOU  KNOW?

In Maricopa County there is a small peak, 742 feet high, called Squaw Tits Summit.

Under Arizona Law...

☛ Under Arizona law (13-3208), a person who knowingly is an employee at a house of prostitution or a prostitution enterprise is guilty of a Class-1 misdemeanor, while a person who knowingly operates or maintains a house of prostitution or a prostitution enterprise is guilty of a Class-5 felony.

☛ Under Arizona law (13-1422), "An adult arcade, adult bookstore or video store, adult cabaret, adult motion picture theater, adult theater, escort agency or nude model studio shall not remain open at any time between the hours of 1:00 AM and 8:00 AM on Monday through Saturday and between the hours of 1:00 AM and 12:00 noon on Sunday."

☛ Under Arizona law (13-1408), adultery is a Class-3 misdemeanor.

Transvestites

Looking to the southwest from Phoenix, you can see the Sierra Estrella Mountains, and the highest of those peaks was known by the Maricopa Indians as *Vee Al'yaxa,* "Transvestite Mountain," because the only way Coyote was able to avoid the wrath of God—after playing a prank that God didn't think was the least bit funny—was to run to the top of that peak and put on a woman's dress.

DID YOU KNOW?

On March 31, 1991, former child star Danny Bonaduce (Danny Partridge on *The Partridge Family* television show), was arrested in Phoenix for having assaulted a transvestite hooker. Bonaduce explained to the authorities that, being drunk, he hadn't realized that she was a he.

DOLLARS AND CENTS

Arizona's economy was long said to depend on "the 5 C's"—Cotton, Copper, Climate, Cattle and Citrus. While all five remain important, dozens of new industries have now joined them in defining the state's economy. For example, agriculture (including cotton, cattle and citrus) is a $9.2-billion industry in Arizona today—but the restaurant industry here is $7.4 billion, high-tech is $6.2 billion, golf is a $3.5-billion industry in Arizona, and Native American casinos generate $1.94 billion.

Cost of Living

A big reason so many people move to Arizona is that the cost of living in Phoenix or Tucson is very reasonable in comparison to other places.

	A	B	C	D	E	F	G
Anchorage	128.8	133.1	140.3	114.1	105.2	132.2	128.5
Boston	134.7	120.0	164.0	129.2	104.7	136.0	126.8
Los Angeles	144.6	111.8	251.2	78.6	113.5	103.8	103.8
Phoenix	100.6	100.5	100.9	93.6	100.7	101.0	102.4
Tucson	100.3	105.4	95.9	96.3	100.5	102.3	102.7

100 is the national average (2007). A = composite index (100%), B = grocery items (13%), C = housing (28%), D = utilities (10%), E = transportation (10%), F = health-care (4%), G = miscellaneous (35%).

Nuclear Utilities

The largest nuclear power plant in the United States is located in Wintersburg, Arizona, 45 miles west of downtown Phoenix: the Palo Verde Nuclear Generating Station, which supplies electricity to more than four million people in Central Arizona and Southern California. The plant took 12 years to build, cost $5.9 billion, and opened in 1988. Palo Verde has about 2500 employees. Wintersburg has about 2500 residents.

GENERAL ECONOMIC INFORMATION

Gross Domestic Product vs. Gross National Product (2006)

Arizona:	$232,463,000,000
Ireland:	$222,080,000,000
Thailand:	$206,558,000,000
Hong Kong:	$189,538,000,000
United Arab Emirates:	$168,263,000,000
Israel:	$140,195,000,000
Egypt:	$107,375,000,000

GDP = the value of all goods and services produced in a state or country during one year; GNP = the value of all goods and services produced by the citizens of a country (including those residing in other countries) during one year.

Tax Burden

The tax burden in Arizona—that is, state and local taxes as a percentage of income—is comfortably halfway between the highest tax burden and the lowest in the nation.

Vermont (highest):	14.1%
Arizona:	10.3%
Alaska (lowest):	6.6%

Sales Tax

In its sales tax, Arizona ranks tenth highest, meaning it's in the upper fifth of all states.

1. Tennessee 9.35%

2. Louisiana 8.70%

3. Washington 8.45%

4. New York 8.25%

5. Oklahoma 8.15%

6. Alabama 8.00%

7. Arkansas 8.00%

8. California 7.95%

9. Texas 7.95%

10. Arizona 7.80%

JOBS AND UNEMPLOYMENT

Work and Play

Although to plenty of people Arizona is a great place to play, or at least not work, 45 percent of the state's population goes to work every day.

Arizona population (2007):	6,338,775
Arizona civilian labor force:	2,884,000
U.S. unemployment rate (2006):	4.6%
Arizona unemployment rate (2006):	4.1%

Arizona's Top Employers (2006)

Private Sector

Employer	Business	Employees
Wal-Mart	discount stores	25,000
Banner Health	hospitals	19,000
Wells Fargo	financial services	11,000
Intel	semiconductors	10,000
Honeywell	aerospace	10,000
Raytheon	missiles	10,000
Bashas'	supermarkets	9000
Home Depot	home improvement	9000
Kroger	grocery stores	9000
JP Morgan Chase	financial services	9000

Public Sector

Employer	Business	Employees
State of Arizona	government	60,000
Maricopa County	government	14,000
Pima County	government	10,000

Military

Employer	Business	Employees
Fort Huachuca	army	16,000
Davis-Monthan	air force	10,000
Luke	air force	7500

The Bottom Line

Personal income in Arizona rose at a slower rate between 2006 and 2007 than any other state. Arizona's per capita income (2008) is $33,029—up 3.4 percent from the prior year, compared to a 5.2 percent increase nationwide. Overall, Arizona now ranks 40th in the nation in personal income growth.

Millionaires Galore

With 126,394 "millionaire households" (according to *The Wall Street Journal*, May 8, 2008), Maricopa County ranks third in the nation for millionaire households. That total number of households far from the poverty line is growing fast: Maricopa County added 23,000 new millionaire households in 2007—that's 63 per day.

Paradise Valley is a "millionaires-only type of town." The Arizona community with the most millionaires? Arrowhead Ranch, in Metro Phoenix.

Bankrupt!

In 2005, there were 40,214 bankruptcies in Arizona, only 525 of them business filings, the rest, 39,689 (or 98.70 percent), being personal bankruptcies. This is comparable to other Western states. For example, personal bankruptcies accounted for 97.46 percent of the total bankruptcies in California for that same year.

THREE GREAT IDEAS FOR TRANSPORTATION

Riverboats

From 1852 to 1909, sternwheeler riverboats, identical to the ones that plied the Mississippi River, made regular trips from Port Isabel in the Gulf of California up the Colorado River, supplying military outposts and supporting commerce throughout the area. The first steamboat on the river, *Uncle Sam,* carried 35 tons of supplies.

Trains

The first locomotive in Arizona was Southern Pacific No. 31—the first to cross the Colorado River into Arizona. The date was September 30, 1877. From then until 1909, when the Age of the Automobile began, trains ruled transportation in Arizona. The Grand Canyon Railway made its first journey to the Grand Canyon on September 17, 1901. Those who have ridden the Grand Canyon Railway include four Presidents—Theodore Roosevelt, William Howard Taft, Franklin Delano Roosevelt, and Dwight D. Eisenhower—and plenty of famous people, including Clark Gable, Doris Day, comedian Jimmy Durante, Sierra Club founder John Muir, Warren Buffet and Bill Gates. You can still ride the old Grand Canyon Railway, between Williams and the South Rim.

The McCormick-Stillman Railroad Park, located in the heart of Scottsdale, is the most unique park of its kind in the country. In addition to miniature trains to ride there is a splendid collection of historic railroad cars. One is the Roald Amundsen Pullman Car. Built in 1928, this car provided maximum security and was used at various times by every president from Herbert Hoover to Dwight D. Eisenhower. It was in this car on

August 18, 1940, in Ogdensburg, New York, that President Franklin Delano Roosevelt and Canadian Prime Minister W.L. Mackenzie King signed the Ogdensburg Declaration, an agreement that created NORAD for the joint defense of North America. The car was donated to the park in 1971.

Stagecoaches

The most famous of many stagecoach outfits was the Butterfield Stage, which ran 250 coaches on a route that had 139 relay stations. The route was from St. Louis through Arkansas and Texas to Arizona (to Tucson, then to Yuma), then to Los Angeles and finally to San Francisco: 2795 miles in 22 days, for a one-way fare of $200. The old stagecoach routes later essentially became the network over which Arizona's modern state highway system was developed.

DID YOU KNOW?

The leather baggage compartment at the rear of the stagecoach was called the boot. The stagecoach driver's seat was the box. Reins were called lines or ribbons. Drivers were called "Charlie" or, from a biblical character who drove fast and furiously, "Jehu." The two horses closest to the stage were the wheelers, and the two in front were the leaders.

TWO TERRIBLE IDEAS FOR TRANSPORTATION

Camels

The use of camels for transport through the Arizona desert *seemed* like a great idea. So did the Pony Express.

When Jefferson Davis was Secretary of War under President Franklin Pierce (1853–57), he approved a plan to use camels for freighting and communication in the arid Southwest. Ships were sent to the Middle East and brought back 74 camels, the first group arriving on February 10, 1856. With them came a camel expert, an Arab named Hadji Ali, who was promptly dubbed "Hi Jolly" by the Arizona cowboys.

The experiment was a disaster. Camels are not known for a pleasant disposition, and cowboys kept shooting them when they spooked their horses. Finally, the surviving camels were turned loose in the Arizona desert. Contrary to today's urban legend, there is no law making it illegal to hunt camels in Arizona—but there used to be. Although sightings were reported into the 1950s, camels were declared extinct here in 1913. Hi Jolly remained here, and died on December 16, 1902. He was buried in Quartzsite (La Paz County), and you can see his tomb there today.

Pony Express

Books, movies and popular reenactments have kept the old mail delivery system called the Pony Express alive and well in America's imagination, but it was a complete failure. The Pony Express began on April 3, 1860, and was closed down on October 26, 1861. In those 19 months, the company grossed $91,000 and lost $240,000. When they first advertised the service—faster mail delivery from St. Joseph, Missouri, through Arizona, to Sacramento, California—the owners printed up a poster that was plastered all over the country to recruit Pony Express riders. That poster read, "Wanted: Young, skinny, wiry fellows not over 18. Must be expert riders willing to risk death daily. Orphans preferred."

DID YOU KNOW?

Since 1958, volunteers of the Hashknife Pony Express have delivered mail once each year, riding the 200 miles from Holbrook to Scottsdale every January. The arrival of 30 riders bearing roughly 20,000 first-class letters (each hand-stamped "Via Pony Express") kicks off Scottsdale's biggest annual parade, the Parada del Sol.

Only two places in the United States today still have postal workers who ride a mule to deliver the mail, and both of them are in the Grand Canyon: Havasu Falls, where the Havasupai tribe has lived for 800 years; and Phantom Ranch, a resort village founded in 1922.

CARS, ROADS AND TRAFFIC

Arizona became a state, in 1912, just as the Age of the Automobile was getting underway. Automobile ownership in the United States went from a grand total of four vehicles in 1894 to nearly 27 million by 1930. Traffic service and control followed cars. White lines first appeared on American roads the year Arizona became a state, in 1912.

Interstate Highways in Arizona

(even numbers run east/west; odd numbers run north/south)

I-8
- Casa Grande to Yuma—main route to San Diego

- Miles in Arizona: 178

I-10
- "The Papago Freeway," or "The Maricopa Freeway"

- Across the southern and central parts of the state, through both Tucson and Phoenix

- Miles in Arizona: 392

I-15
- Across the extreme northwest corner of the state—north of the Grand Canyon

- Miles in Arizona: 29

I-17
- "The Black Canyon Freeway"

- Flagstaff to Phoenix

- Miles in Arizona: 146

I-19

☛ Located entirely within Arizona: Tucson to Nogales

☛ Miles total: 63

I-40

☛ Across the northern part of the state, through Flagstaff—
essentially the old Route 66

☛ Miles in Arizona: 359

DID YOU KNOW?

In Territorial days, Black Canyon Hill was a "one way" grade.
Stagecoach drivers waited for each other at certain turnouts,
then blew a horn as a warning that they were coming. That hill
route is now part of Interstate 17, the Black Canyon Freeway—
and people only blow horns when slowpokes won't get out of
the way.

The Mother Road

Route 66 was called "The Main Street of America," "The
Mother Road" (so named by John Steinbeck in *The Grapes of
Wrath*), and "The Will Rogers Highway." Frank Lloyd Wright
said, "Route 66 is a giant chute down which everything loose in
this country is sliding into southern California." The route led
from Gallup, New Mexico, into northern Arizona—through the
Petrified Forest, then through Holbrook, Winslow, Two Guns,
Twin Arrows, Seligman and Kingman—and finally into
California.

State Roads, Traffic, Driving and Accidents

Today Arizona has a 6200-mile state highway system. Statewide in 2006, Arizona vehicles traveled 87,212,000 miles daily. According to a 2008 road rage survey by Auto Vantage, an auto club, Phoenix ranks eighth in the nation for having the least courteous drivers. (The nation's least courteous drivers are in Miami; the most courteous drivers are in Pittsburgh.) Some Arizona traffic accident statistics (2006):

- ☛ Annual economic loss $3.67 billion
- ☛ Crashes during daylight hours   71.9%
- ☛ Most fatal hour   7:00–8:00 PM
- ☛ Most fatal day   Saturday
- ☛ Worst month for crashes   October
- ☛ Most common crash   rear-end
- ☛ One person injured every   7.67 minutes
- ☛ Total crashes   1121

- Urban crashes   519
- Rural crashes   602
- Alcohol-related crashes   42%
- Fatalities (vehicles)   1177
- Pedestrians killed   170
- Bicyclists killed   29
- Motorcyclists killed   155

Traffic Hazard: Elk

Arizona drivers who collide with elk each year: approx. 600

Arizona drivers killed in collisions with elk each year: approx. 5

Arizona elk killed in collisions with cars each year: approx. 600

Elk bulls weigh 700 pounds, and elk cows weigh 500 pounds, and in a collision the vehicle is almost always damaged or destroyed. In December 1998, Jerry Booth was driving on I-40 near Flagstaff when he crashed into the carcass of an elk that had been hit by another motorist and left on the highway. Booth sustained serious injuries in the crash and sued the state for not keeping the freeway clear. A jury in 2004 awarded Booth $3 million, and the appeals court upheld the verdict.

DID YOU KNOW?

Arizona ranks first in the nation for auto theft. About 50,000 vehicles are stolen each year—which works out to 137 stolen every day. Nearly two-thirds are returned to owners, which means that about 20,000 each year are not located or returned. Economic loss: $377 million each year.

TAKING TO THE AIR

Arizona's Aerospace and Defense Commission was created only recently, in 2004, but this state has led the nation in aviation for almost a century. During World War II, the Army Air Corps ran bombing training flights at the airports in Kingman, Holbrook, Flagstaff, Winslow and Tucson. Why Arizona? Partly it was the perfect flying weather, but mostly it was Arizona's already long aviation history.

America's First Municipal Airport

In 1919, just 16 years after the Wright brothers' flight at Kitty Hawk—during which their aircraft flew at 6.8 miles per hour— the first commercial airport in the United States opened, in Tucson. That airport today is Tucson International Airport, where, as at all other big airports, passengers moving through security think 6.8 miles per hour is really fast.

Lucky Lindy Landed Here

Four months after Charles Lindbergh, "Lucky Lindy," became the first man ever to solo over the Atlantic on May 21, 1927, he flew the same plane, the Spirit of St. Louis, almost the same distance west, to Tucson, where he dedicated Davis-Monthan Airport, at the time the largest municipal airport in the United States. That airport was frequently used by other aviation pioneers, among them Amelia Earhart and Jimmy Doolittle. Davis-Monthan was acquired by the U.S. Air Force in 1940.

Aircraft Boneyard

In 2600 acres adjacent to Davis-Monthan Air Force Base is the Aerospace Maintenance and Regeneration Group (AMARC), or "the Boneyard." Nearly 5000 obsolete or mothballed military aircraft dating from World War II to the present are parked there, and hundreds are visible from the I-10 freeway between Tucson and Phoenix. To put that number in perspective, if those 5000 aircraft were activated, they would be the third largest air force in the world. The nearby Pima Air and Space Museum offers tours of Davis-Monthan's AMARC.

Classes in the Sky

Known as "the Harvard of the Skies," Embry-Riddle Aeronautical University is widely regarded as the best flight school in the world, and is the world's only accredited aviation university. With West and East campuses in Prescott, Arizona, and Daytona Beach, Florida, Embry-Riddle graduates one of every four pilots who fly commercially in the United States. More than a dozen American astronauts learned to fly there, as did Scott O'Grady, the U.S.A.F. pilot who in 1995 evaded capture after his F-16 was shot down in Bosnia.

FOUR UNIQUE BUSINESSES

Apiculture

Apiculture (beekeeping) in Arizona is valued at $11.8 million annually. Southern Arizona has nearly 1200 different species of bees (not a single one native to Arizona), and the Carl Hayden Bee Research Center, located in Tucson, assists commercial bee-keepers by conducting research in honey bee nutrition, Varroa mites (which kill bees), the Africanization of European honey bees, and crop pollination.

Trading Posts

For more than a century in Arizona, "doing business" and "going shopping" meant taking a trip to the trading post. Most trading posts today are located in northeast Arizona, including the Hubbell Trading Post, the oldest continuously operating trading post in the Navajo Nation. Opened in 1878 and still open, the Hubbell (no relation to the Hubbell telescope) is now a National Historic Site. It's one mile west of Ganado, Arizona, and 55 miles northwest of Gallup, New Mexico. Arizona's other best trading posts today:

☞ Cameron: Cameron Trading Post (established 1929)

☞ Kykotsmovi: Sockyma's Arts & Crafts

☞ Kykotsmovi: Tsu-Kurs-Ovi

☞ Old Oraibi: Monongya Gallery

☞ Second Mesa: Badger Arts & Crafts

☞ Second Mesa: Honani Gallery

☞ Second Mesa: Hopi Arts & Crafts Guild

☞ Second Mesa: Hopi Gallery

☞ Second Mesa: Is-Ka-Sok-Pu

☞ Second Mesa: Shalako Arts & Crafts

☞ Second Mesa: The Hopi Cultural Center

Sightseeing Aviation

All over the state there are companies ready to fly you all over the state, by helicopter or small plane. In the Grand Canyon, Monument Valley, Sedona, and everywhere else, the bird's-eye view is more awesome than the worm's-eye view. Sightseeing aviation in Arizona got a turbo-boost in 1987 when Ray Bluff Jr. set up Red Rock Aviation. That first year, he sold 40,000 gallons of aviation fuel; within five years, he was selling that much fuel per month. Nationwide, the industry averages 1.9 accidents per 100,000 hours flown, which is a quarter of the number of accidents of private planes, but 10 times greater than commercial aircraft. All of the sightseeing helicopter accidents in the United States since 1996 have occurred in just four states: Hawaii (20 accidents), Arizona (10), Alaska (8) and New York (1). Leading sightseeing aviation companies in Arizona include:

- Glendale: Gold Coast Helicopters, Vertical Airborne Helicopters

- Grand Canyon: Airstar Helicopters

- Litchfield Park: Aerial Systems

- Mesa: Arizona Heliservices

- Phoenix: Aero-Helicopters of Arizona, U.S. Helicopters

- Scottsdale: Premier Helicopters, Scottsdale Helicopters, Westcor Aviation

- Tucson: Voyager Flight Services

Have Goat, Will Travel

So you're the kind of person who loves long hikes in just about any kind of backcountry, but you're tired of toting all the supplies you need for overnights in the wilderness. Let's face it: big, bulky backpacks have a way of hindering our photo-taking abilities. As it happens, Tom and Teri DiMaggio were struggling with the same frustration when they established Purple Mountain Pack Goats of Tucson. The company organizes day hikes, overnight outings and educational field trips, and outfits these expeditions with male goats called "wethers." These wethers, which are able to carry about 50–75 pounds, hike along at about the same speed as their human counterparts and can travel up to 10 miles a day. So if you're into hiking with a difference, check out the DiMaggios.

AMAZING
ARIZONA

In 1860, a Pole named Mike Goldwasser arrived in Arizona and started selling knives, tobacco, belts, shoes, ammunition and epaulets for army officers. Nearly four decades later, he changed his name, and in 1896, with his sons Morris and Baron, he opened M. Goldwater & Sons. Soon Goldwater's was the most prestigious store in Phoenix, and at statehood in 1912 it was Arizona's leading department store. Baron's son Barry Goldwater became a U.S. senator and the 1964 Republican presidential candidate.

MAJOR INDUSTRIES

Leading the Nation

Industries in which Arizona ranked first in the nation in 2002:

Industry*	Total sales or receipts
Consumer lending	$4,701,479,000
Truck, utility trailer and RV rental and leasing	$615,835,000
Truss manufacturing	$223,584,000
Concrete block and brick manufacturing	$183,825,000
Other transit and ground passenger transportation	$106,342,000
All other transit and ground passenger transportation	$50,371,000

*Industry names according to the North American Industry Classification System (NAICS).

Second in Dining

In 2006, Arizona ranked second in the nation in terms of dining industry sales and restaurant job growth, behind Nevada. Statewide sales in Arizona: $7.4 billion. The National Restaurant Association reports that 233,900 Arizonans are employed in the food service industry, a number that is expected to grow to nearly 300,000 by 2015, a 26.5 percent growth rate.

DID YOU  KNOW?

Arizona is not an "oil state"—but an oil derrick began operation in Chino Valley on October 24, 1917. It was soon abandoned.

The Military

The military has a major impact on Arizona's economy. Our facilities range in size from less than 100 acres to over two million acres and are:

☛ Air Force Research Laboratory, Mesa Research Site (Williams Gateway)

☛ Arizona Air National Guard, Phoenix Sky Harbor International Airport

☛ Arizona Air National Guard, Tucson International Airport

☛ Barry M. Goldwater Range (including Gila Bend Air Force Auxiliary Field)

☛ Camp Navajo (Arizona Army National Guard)

☛ Davis-Monthan Air Force Base

☛ Florence Military Reservation (Arizona Army National Guard)

☛ Fort Huachuca (including Libby Army Airfield)

☛ Luke Air Force Base (including Luke Auxiliary Field #1)

☛ Marine Corps Air Station (MCAS) Yuma

☛ Papago Park Military Reservation (Arizona Army National Guard)

☛ Silverbell Army Heliport

☛ United States Naval Observatory, Flagstaff Station

☛ U.S. Army Yuma Proving Ground

AGRICULTURE

Arizona has 7500 farms and ranches, and a $9.2 billion agricultural industry. From apples to zucchini, approximately 100 different types and varieties of fruits and vegetables are grown in the state. Arizona-grown fresh fruits and vegetables are available every month of the year.

Grown to Wear

In cotton production, Arizona ranks second in the nation in Pima cotton, ninth in production of upland cotton, and eight in production of cottonseed. The state grows enough cotton each year to make a pair of jeans for every man, woman and child in the United States. Meanwhile, Arizona cattle ranchers supply enough cattle hides each year to manufacture 17 million pairs of men's shoes.

Grown to Eat

☛ Vegetables—Arizona's top fresh-produce commodity is lettuce, with $590 million in cash receipts in 2004. Arizona ranks second in the nation in the production of head lettuce, leaf lettuce, romaine lettuce, cauliflower and broccoli. Yuma is the winter lettuce capital of the world.

☛ Fruits—Arizona ranks second in the production of cantaloupes and lemons, third in the production of tangerines and honeydew melons, fourth in orange and grapefruit production, fifth in the nation in watermelon production and sixth in grapes. Arizona apple growers produce 94.5 million pounds of apples each year.

☛ Nuts—Arizona has 15,242 acres producing pecans and 2500 acres producing pistachios. Arizona's annual pistachio production is valued at $5.14 million.

- Wheat—Arizona ranks second in the nation in production of durum wheat, producing 257,000 tons annually.

- Beef—Beef is Arizona's leading agricultural product. Arizona ranchers produce enough beef annually—830,000 head—to feed over 4.6 million Americans. In Stanfield (Pinal County), the Red Eye Ranch was almost as famous for its beef as it was for its owner: actor John Wayne.

- Dairy—The 140,000 dairy cows in Arizona have a yearly milk production average of 21,705 pounds—10.85 tons per cow. Approximately 5.9 million gallons of ice cream are made from Arizona milk annually, which is roughly 1.5 gallons of ice cream for every man, woman, and child in the state. Tucson is home to Shamrock Farms, the largest family-owned and -operated dairy in the Southwest. Shamrock was founded by W.T. McClelland and his wife Winifred in 1922 with little more than "20 cows, a Model T delivery truck, and one route man delivering fresh milk to the doorsteps of local customers."

THE HEALTHY PLACE

Calling All Sick People

Since Territorial days, Arizona has been a magnet for health-seekers. After getting tuberculosis back east, Doc Holliday came to Arizona, and the move added 15 years to his life. Civil War veteran Winfield Scott's old battle wounds hurt, so he left San Diego, traveled to Arizona and ended up founding Scottsdale. Connecticut freight operator and merchant Charles Hayden suffered a lung ailment, so he moved to Arizona and ended up founding Tempe. After 1870, special health facilities began to open throughout the state. Near Prescott, for example, an "Emergency Relief Administration Health Camp" for girls operated in Granite Dells. The state's clean, dry air also attracted people suffering from allergies and lung ailments, and Arizona soon became known nationwide as an especially healthy place. Packaging health Western-style, guest ranches also sprang up throughout the state. Eventually those ranches gave way to today's numerous luxurious resorts and health spas.

Dudes

Originally in Arizona, sickly visitors were viewed as fools, from the Irish slang term for a foolish person, *dud*—the origin of the more generic Arizona term for any city slicker who is ignorant of Western ways: dude. To welcome the hordes of Easterners who wanted to experience the cowboy lifestyle in the 1920s and '30s, "dude ranches" were built all over Arizona, some of which were the Tanque Verde and the Flying V in Tucson, the Wigwam in Phoenix and the K.L. Bar and Remuda in Wickenburg. In 1936 the Jay-Six Ranch, outside Benson, hired a 19-year-old from Boston who wanted to work as a ranch hand that summer: John F. Kennedy.

Natural Remedies Galore

In the 21st century, people everywhere are discovering what Arizonans knew for centuries: natural remedies are great for health and wellness. The Yuma Indians used *hu'upa* (mesquite leaves) for headaches and ate mesquite pods for sore throats. For stomach troubles, the Pima ate a gruel made of cholla buds. They and the Tohono O'odham (Papago) chewed *segoi* (creosote gum) for dysentery, and Mexican Americans drank *hediondilla* (creosote tea) for kidney problems, infections and abdominal pains. Chinese Americans in Arizona, arriving with the railroads after 1877, used medicines made from over 3000 plant and animal ingredients, including fennel for hernias or eye catarrhs and ginseng root for everything from insomnia to impotence to the infirmities of old age.

Many Native American tribes placed a sliced-open prickly pear pad on cuts, bruises, burns and other open sores, and also treated diabetes with prickly pear. Mexican Americans used *ajo* (garlic) for high blood pressure and to treat insect bites. Arizona pioneers wore garlic around their necks to ward off colds. Mexican Americans used dry cholla stems to make casts for fractures. The Tohono O'odham used rumex root as a disinfectant, and the Yuma gave *kau vattai* (wild rhubarb) to teething babies. The Yuma also used *kovanao* (creosote) for foot odor.

LIFE EXPECTANCY

Youthful Arizona

Despite the state's reputation as a retirement center, the population is slightly younger than the national average: Arizona's median age is 34.4 years while the nation's is 34.9.

Golden Oldies

According to an Arizona Health Status and Vital Statistics report for 2006, Arizonans can expect to live to about 76 years of age. Nationwide in 2005, the life expectancy of men was 75.2 years and that of women was 80.4 years.

Suicide

Arizona's teen suicide rate is slightly higher than the national average. In 2002, there were 12 suicides in Arizona among 10- to 14-year-olds and 39 suicides in the 15–19 age group. In 2003, there were 86 suicides in the 15–24 age group, 134 among 24- to 35-year-olds and 228 for those 55 and older. Most suicides in Arizona (60 percent) are carried out with a firearm.

Deaths and Births (2005)

County	Deaths	Births	Some Communities in the County
Apache	499	1283	Alpine, Eagar, Greer, Springerville
Cochise	1116	1769	Benson, Douglas, Tombstone, Wilcox
Coconino	632	2070	Flagstaff, Page, Sedona, Tuba City
Gila	690	649	Globe, Payson, San Carlos, Tonto Basin
Graham	282	452	Peridot, Pima, Safford, Thatcher
Greenlee	62	99	Clifton, Duncan, Sheldon, York Valley
La Paz	181	245	Cibola, Ehrenberg, Parker, Poston
Maricopa	24,902	62,232	Apache Junction, Mesa, Phoenix, Tempe
Mohave	2345	2237	Bullhead City, Kingman, Lake Havasu City
Navajo	802	1903	Cibecue, Heber, Kayenta, Show Low
Pima	7948	12,976	Ajo, Green Valley, Oro Valley, Tucson
Pinal	1886	3641	Casa Grande, Florence, Kearny, Superior
Santa Cruz	257	781	Elgin, Nogales, Rio Rico, Tubac
Yavapai	2263	2115	Camp Verde, Cottonwood, Prescott, Williams
Yuma	1246	3292	Gadsden, San Luis, Weldon, Yuma

GENERAL HEALTH AND WELLNESS

Making the Health Grade

A study conducted by HighBeam Research, LLC, put Arizona in the 42nd spot when it came to ranking the country's healthiest states in 2007, down two spots from its 40th place finish in 2006. Arizona is in the middle of the road when it comes to its placing among the country's most livable states, sitting in at the 32nd spot, down from the 2006 ranking of 29th.

Obesity

Arizona has the 40th highest level of adult obesity in the nation at 20.1 percent; the 19th highest overweight levels for high school students at 10.8 percent; and the 30th highest overweight levels for low-income children ages 2–5, at 11.4 percent. The state spent an estimated $135 per person in 2003 on medical costs related to obesity.

Hospitals Were Rare

Modern health care in the U.S. came into being at roughly the same time Arizona became a state (1912). In 1900, there were only 200 hospitals in the entire country (one-third of them psychiatric hospitals); by 1930, America had 7000 hospitals. Opened in Tucson in 1880, St. Mary's Hospital was the first hospital to be built in the Arizona Territory.

Most early Arizona hospitals were small, and many were built by private businesses for their own employees. In Flagstaff in 1920, the Arizona Lumber and Timber Company opened Milton Hospital (also called Mercy Hospital) to treat sawmill workers and their families. It had one operating room, eight beds and two private rooms. Today in Flagstaff you can visit a hospital from those early days: the Coconino County Hospital for the Indigent opened in 1908 to serve the people of northern Arizona. The locals called it the "Poor Farm." A ferocious-looking black bear stood guard at the top of the staircase to protect the spirits of the patients. You can still see that bear, as well as view an early-Arizona iron lung and other medical exhibits, because the Arizona Historical Society acquired the building and in 1963 opened it as the Pioneer Museum.

Flagstaff Medical Center

Also in Flagstaff, a few minutes' drive from the Pioneer Museum, is proof of how far medical care has come in Arizona: the Flagstaff Medical Center (FMC). Opened in 1936 with 25 beds, the FMC is one of the finest hospitals and regional trauma centers in the United States today. In 2006 at the FMC:

Beds	270
Physicians on active medical staff	190
Inpatient hospital visits	12,061
Outpatient hospital visits	34,699
Emergency room visits	38,403
Babies born	1652

Other Great Facilities

State-of-the-art medical care is also found in central and southern Arizona. When the world-famous Mayo Clinic in Minnesota wanted to expand, they built one campus in Phoenix and a second one in Scottsdale (and a third in Florida). In 2003, the University Medical Center in Tucson became the first hospital in Arizona to win the so-called Nobel Prize for Nursing—the Magnet Hospital designation that is the American Nurses Association's highest national honor for nursing excellence.

Hospitals and Medical Care Facilities (2007)

County	Number of Facilities	County	Number of Facilities
Apache	7	Mohave	4
Cochise	13	Navajo	9
Coconino	11	Pima	34
Gila	4	Pinal	9
Graham	2	Santa Cruz	4
Greenlee	1	Yavapai	13
La Paz	4	Yuma	8
Maricopa	83		

Medical Schools

Founded in 1967, the College of Medicine at the University of Arizona in Tucson was the first college of medicine in Arizona. In 2006, the U of A's College of Medicine Phoenix program opened the Phoenix Biomedical Campus in collaboration with Arizona State University.

MEDICAL PROFESSIONALS

The Physician Governor

For the 36 years from 1897 to 1933, Benjamin Baker Moeur delivered virtually all of the babies born in Tempe. The good doctor then went into politics. A Democrat, Moeur became Arizona's eighth governor, and almost every day during the four years of his term (1933–37), he conducted free medical clinics in the capitol rotunda during his lunch hour.

Early Healers

In the 1890s, when the average American worker earned $10 per week, doctors charged $3 for an office visit and $6 for a house call. But there weren't many doctors or doctor offices in Arizona, and people relied, as they had for centuries, on professional healers. For childbirth, Anglos and African Americans in Arizona called on midwives to assist them. For other aches and pains, Mexican Americans sought medical help from a *curandero* or *curandera*, Yuma Indians from a *hitevi*, Papago Indians from a *ma'kai* and Chinese Americans from an herbalist. By 1900, there were three Chinese herbalist businesses in Tucson. Today in Tucson, there is the Arizona School of Acupuncture and Oriental Medicine.

Healers Today

In 2000, Arizona ranked 33rd among states in physicians per capita, with 172 physicians per 100,000 people compared to a national average of 198. In 2000, there were 628 nurses per 100,000 people in Arizona, compared to a national average of 782. Arizona ranked 41st in the nation in the number of dentists: 44 per 100,000 people compared to 63.6 nationally. Arizona ranked third in the nation in the number of chiropractors.

Two of Many Great Arizona Doctors

In 1960, just four years out of medical school in Chicago, Donald F. Schaller, M.D., of Phoenix performed the first open heart surgery in Arizona. After retiring as a thoracic and cardio-vascular surgeon, he founded a medical and dental clinic at the Society of St. Vincent de Paul in 1992. Today, the clinic has 110 doctors and 35 dentists, all volunteers, who provide care to an estimated 12,000 low-income people each year. In 1972, Dr. Schaller co-founded the Arizona Health Plan, a precursor to CIGNA HealthCare of Arizona. In 1984, he was appointed by Governor Bruce Babbitt to head the state's Medicaid program (the Arizona Health Care Cost Containment System)—the nation's first statewide Medicaid program based on man-aged care.

An orthopedic surgeon at the Flagstaff Medical Center, John W. Durham, M.D., was voted Arizona's Physician of the Year in 2005. He received his training at the University of Vermont School of Medicine and completed his internship and residency at the Albany Medical College in New York and the Iowa Hospital and Clinics in Iowa City. Dr. Durham has a great passion for his work, because being a physician is something he always wanted to do. "I knew ever since I was in high school that I wanted to be a doctor," he said on receiving the award in 2005, "My family doctor was a wonderful man, and inspired me in many ways." Durham (along with podiatrist Kelly Reber) is a member of the Northern Arizona Volunteer Medical and Surgical Corporation, a team of doctors who have been traveling to a small clinic in Nuevo Casas Grandes in Chihuahua since 1991 to bring free medical care to the poor in Mexico. "Besides being doctors, they are men whose value is gold," said Carmen Escudero, a patient's wife, in 2005.

Pharmacists

Until fairly recently, home remedies and folk medicines were common in Arizona, and for a long time quack medicines were everywhere—most of them were "scientifically prepared," but few of them were actually helpful. There were no drug stores or pharmacies. At Arizona general stores and trading posts, people bought oils, bitters, tonics and balms for everything from "brain fatigue" to "torpid liver." There are pharmacists here today—but *very* few of them. With only 2150 pharmacists in 2000, Arizona ranked 50th in the nation in the number of pharmacists per 100,000 people.

READING AND WRITING...USUALLY

Best and Worst

Arizona has 220 local school districts, and the tale of education in the state's cities is aptly described in the opening line of *A Tale of Two Cities,* by Charles Dickens: "It was the best of times, it was the worst of times, it was the age of wisdom, it was the age of foolishness." In 2008 a Tucson school, Basis Charter, placed first in the nation in *Newsweek* magazine's poll of America's best public schools. But in the same poll, a Phoenix school, North Pointe Prep, placed 1281st, and in a different poll in 2007 that ranked "the Smartest States" in terms of 21 educational factors, Arizona placed 50th, dead last.

Notable Graduates

Among the "products" of Arizona schools are some pretty famous people:

- director Steven Spielberg (Ingleside Elementary School and Arcadia High School, in Phoenix)

- Lynda "Wonder Woman" Carter (Arcadia High School)

- singer Wayne Newton (North Phoenix High School)

- rock star Alice Cooper (Washington Elementary School, Cortez High School, Phoenix)

- actor Nick Nolte takes the "Schooled in Arizona" crown—he attended Arizona State University in Tempe, Eastern Arizona College in Thatcher and Phoenix College in Phoenix

Literacy Today

In 2005, 35 percent of Arizona's eighth graders read significantly below grade level, compared with a national average of 29 percent. Of particular concern to Arizona educators was the achievement gap between white students and Hispanic, Native American and African American students. Arizona's Instrument to Measure Standards (AIMS) showed 15 percent of the state's white eighth graders read below the standard, but the figure rose to 50 percent of Native American students, 38 percent of Hispanic students and 35 percent of African American students. (White students comprised 49 percent of Arizona's public school enrollment, Hispanic students 37 percent, Native American students seven percent, African American students five percent and Asian American students two percent.)

DID YOU KNOW?

Arizona ranks second highest in the United States in the rate of teen pregnancies, and teen pregnancy contributes to Arizona having one of the lowest high-school graduation rates in the nation.

Literacy Tomorrow

☛ In Arizona, literacy as a goal is both general and specialized. There are general "literacy" programs, "adolescent literacy" programs and "adult literacy" programs. Hundreds of other groups also promote general literacy throughout Arizona such as the Phoenix West Reading Council, which was chartered in 1972. An affiliate of the Arizona Reading Association (ARA) and the International Reading Association (IRA), Phoenix West now serves individuals in more than 500 public, private and charter schools, libraries and colleges.

☛ To promote literacy statewide, Governor Janet Napolitano began a Free Book Program in 2003, providing a new book to every first grader throughout the state. In 2005, the program was expanded to include a book for every fourth grader. More than one million free books were given to Arizona students since the start of the program. The program is funded through private sponsorship by McDonald's, HSBC–North America, Arizona Public Service, the Helios Education Foundation, Freeport-McMoRan Copper & Gold, Inc. (formerly Phelps Dodge) and other corporations and organizations.

☛ Then there are the specialized literacy programs for everything from "technological literacy" (such as AT LAST—Achieving Technological Literacy in Arizona for Students and Teachers) to "environmental literacy" (AAEE—Arizona Association for Environmental Education) to "science literacy" (SAMEC—Science and Math Education Center, at the University of Arizona in Tucson) to "financial literacy" (Arizona Jump$tart Coalition for Personal Financial Literacy) to "economic literacy" (ACEE—Arizona Council for Economic Education).

Top International School in the World

In 1939, Hollywood star Jimmy Stewart and a few of his friends pooled their money and built an airfield near Glendale, Arizona, to train American and Canadian fliers for World War II. Stewart called it Thunderbird Field. After the war, right near that field, a school was built in 1946 that no one on earth had ever seen: a graduate school specializing in international management and global business. In tribute to Jimmy's airfield, it's called the Thunderbird School of Global Management, or just Thunderbird. The first and oldest school of its kind, Thunderbird is also far and away the best—*The Wall Street Journal, US News & World Report, The Financial Times* and other publications consistently rank it the best in the world. And now the school itself spans the world: still headquartered in Glendale, Thunderbird has branch campuses in Beijing (China), Geneva (Switzerland), Monterrey (Mexico) and Prague (the Czech Republic).

Oldest Schools

☛ Arizona's first school was opened in Tubac the year George Washington was elected the first president of the United States: 1789.

☛ The oldest school still standing in Arizona is in Strawberry (Gila County): the log structure was built in 1885 by a settler named Charles C. Callaway.

☛ Built in 1898, Old Main is Arizona State University's first and oldest building that is still in use. One of the largest buildings ever constructed in the Arizona Territory, the Old Main was the principal academic and administrative center of the campus until the late 1940s, when the post-war expansion of the campus began. The building is distinctive in its use of materials, especially native granite from nearby Tempe Butte and red sandstone from Flagstaff. In March 1911, Theodore Roosevelt spoke from the front steps while visiting Arizona to dedicate Roosevelt Dam.

☛ The University of Arizona also has an Old Main building, and it was used for the first time on October 1, 1891—six freshmen and 26 preparatory students were in that first class. The building is still in use at the U of A, which in 2006 had 36,805 students.

Thank the Gamblers!

The University of Arizona was approved by the Arizona Territorial Legislature and awarded to Tucson in 1885. But when no local resident offered to provide land for the new university, Tucson prepared to return the money to the Legislature. Then two gamblers and a saloonkeeper stepped forward to donate the land necessary to build the school.

DID YOU KNOW?

University of Arizona graduates include talk-show host/journalist Geraldo Rivera, Hollywood producer Jerry Bruckheimer (*Top Gun, Flashdance, Black Hawk Down*), director John Hughes (*Home Alone, Ferris Bueller's Day Off*) and actor Michael Biehn (*Navy SEALS*).

Two Universities That Used to be Normal
In the 19th century in America, a "normal school" was one that trained high-school graduates to be teachers. Two of Arizona's three major universities began as normal schools:

Founded 1885:	Tempe Normal School
In 1898 changed to:	Territorial Normal School at Tempe
In 1900 changed to:	Normal School of Arizona
In 1903 changed to:	Tempe Normal School of Arizona
In 1925 changed to:	Tempe State Teachers College
In 1929 changed to:	Arizona State Teachers College
In 1945 changed to:	Arizona State College at Tempe
Since 1958:	Arizona State University

Founded 1899:	Northern Arizona Normal School
In 1925 changed to:	Northern Arizona State Teacher's College
In 1929 changed to:	Arizona State Teacher's College at Flagstaff
In 1945 changed to:	Arizona State College at Flagstaff
Since 1966:	Northern Arizona University

AMAZING ARIZONA

The large and growing for-profit education movement in the United States began in Arizona when billionaire John Sperling founded the University of Phoenix in 1976. The U of Phoenix now has 204 campuses and learning centers in 38 states, as well as campuses in Canada (Alberta and British Columbia) and Puerto Rico. With 250,000 students, most of them working adults, the school is the largest private accredited university in North America.

Ottawa University

Ottawa University in Phoenix is not named after the capital of Canada. Both the university and the city were named after the Ottawa Indians, who lived (and still do) near Lake Huron, in Michigan. Ottawa University was founded in Kansas in 1865, and other branches have opened in Arizona (1977), Wisconsin (1992) and Indiana (2002).

Community Colleges

Arizona has 21 community colleges. Some are small, such as Diné College, which serves 1830 students at eight different campuses on the 27,000-square-mile Navajo reserve. Some are huge, such as Pima Community College (PCC), which serves 75,000 Tucson-area students at six campuses and four learning centers. PCC is the third largest multi-campus community college in the United States.

The Ghost of the School Girl

The first school in Phoenix was a four-room adobe building constructed in 1874. On that downtown site was built the Hotel San Carlos, which is still there. The San Carlos was the favorite place to stay for boxing champion Jack Dempsey, Mae West, Marilyn Monroe, Clark Gable, Carole Lombard, Gene Autry and John F. Kennedy. And it was also the favorite place of the ghost of a seven-year-old girl who, hotel employees and guests have sworn, now and then wanders the hotel hallways, still crying that her school was demolished in 1918, right before she died in the great Spanish flu pandemic.

World's Biggest Community College District

The Maricopa Community College District, called the Maricopa Community Colleges, is the biggest community college district in the world: during the 2006–07 school year, it had 269,774 students. In 2006 the Maricopa Community Colleges, headquartered in Tempe, employed nearly 4500 full-time faculty and staff and more than 9000 part-time faculty and staff, at 10 colleges, two skill centers and numerous education centers. The 10 colleges are:

Chandler-Gilbert Community College

Estrella Mountain Community College

Glendale Community College

GateWay Community College

Mesa Community College

Paradise Valley Community College

Phoenix College

Rio Salado Community College

Scottsdale Community College

South Mountain Community College

THE PEOPLE'S PEOPLE

Government at a Glance

☛ Arizona's 15 counties are divided into 30 legislative districts, each of which elects one state senator and two state representatives—30 senators and 60 representatives are in each Legislature.

☛ Arizona has no lieutenant governor (the Secretary of State fulfills that role) and no governor's mansion.

☛ Phoenix adopted a new form of government, from mayor-council to council-manager, in 1913, making it one of the first cities in the U.S. with this form of city government.

Division of Power

As a general rule, Phoenix and Maricopa County vote Republican, while Tucson and Pima County vote Democrat.

Territorial Arizona had 20 different governors and 21 administrations (Nathan Oakes Murphy was the 12th governor and the 17th governor). The State of Arizona has had 21 different governors and 25 administrations. The state's first governor, George W.P. Hunt, was a Democrat who was born in Missouri;

his successor, Thomas Campbell, was a Republican who was born in Prescott—Arizona's first native-born governor. The party breakdown of all 46 gubernatorial administrations is as follows:

	Republican	Democrat
Arizona Territory (1863–1912)	17	4
State of Arizona (1912–2008)	9	16

Women in Government

☞ Arizona has had more female governors (three) than any state in the country and is one of only two states to have elected female governors from both major parties: Democrat Rose Mofford, Republican Jane Dee Hull and Democrat Janet Napolitano.

☞ Suffrage (from the Latin for "the right to vote") wasn't won for women in America until 1920. But the same year as the Gunfight at the O.K. Corral, 1881, Murat Masterson introduced in the Arizona House a bill entitled "To Extend the Right of Suffrage to Women." It was defeated. He reintroduced it in 1883, and again in 1885, and it was defeated both times.

☞ Sharlot Hall was the first woman to hold a salaried office in the Arizona Territory. She served as Territorial Historian from September 1909 to February 1912. In 1914, Apache County sent Rachel Berry to the Arizona House of Representatives, and Yavapai County sent Frances Munds to the Arizona Senate. Munds was only the second female state senator in the nation. A woman has won election to the Arizona House of Representatives every year since 1914.

☞ With a 46-year tenure in the Arizona Legislature, Democrat Polly Rosenbaum was Arizona's longest-serving state representative: 1949–95. She died in 2003, at age 104.

Of the 21 member nations, tribes and councils of the InterTribal Council of Arizona, five are led by women (2008): Delia M. Carlyle, chairwoman of the Ak-Chin Indian Community; Sherry Cordova, chairwoman of the Cocopah Tribe; Ona Segundo, chairwoman of the Kaibab-Paiute Tribe; Diane Enos, president of the Salt River Pima-Maricopa Indian Community; and Mary Lou Boone, president of the San Juan Southern Paiute Tribe.

Land of the Wild Governors

It wasn't just the bad guys who put the "wild" in the Wild West—some of our governors have been pretty wild too.

☛ The administration of Governor Frederick Augustus Tritle (Republican, 1882–85) is remembered for the "Thieving Thirteenth" Legislature in which lawmakers overpaid themselves for fictitious services. During his term, three institutions were created: Arizona State University, University of Arizona in Tucson and the Insane Asylum in Phoenix.

☛ Conrad Zulick (Democrat, 1885–89) was under arrest in Mexico at the time of his appointment as Territorial Governor of Arizona.

☛ Territorial Governor Louis Cameron Hughes (D, 1893–96) hated "demon rum." So he turned down a personal invitation from Teddy Roosevelt to attend the christening of the battleship USS *Arizona,* because a bottle of champagne would be used during the ceremony.

☛ Governor Fife Symington (R, 1991–97) resigned after being convicted of bank fraud, and eventually was pardoned by Bill Clinton.

☛ Governor Evan Mecham (R, 1987–88) was impeached.

☛ Governor Raul Castro (D, 1975–77) resigned to become U.S. Ambassador to Argentina.

☛ Territorial Governor Alexander Brodie (R, 1902–05) resigned to join the U.S. Navy.

☛ Territorial Governor Lewis Wolfley (R, 1889–90) was the Territory's only bachelor governor.

☛ Territorial Governor Anson Safford (R, 1869–77) granted himself a divorce.

☛ Territorial Governor Benjamin Joseph Franklin (D, 1896–97) was a direct descendant of *the* Benjamin Franklin.

☛ Ernest W. McFarland (D) served in the highest position in all three branches of government: Arizona Governor (1955–59), Arizona Supreme Court Justice and U.S. Senator.

☛ George W.P. Hunt (D) was called "George VII" because he served seven terms—which makes him the most elected governor in the history of the United States. Before statehood, he was the first mayor of Globe (Gila County). Then he was the State of Arizona's 1st governor, and its 2nd, and its 3rd, and its 6th, 7th, 8th and 10th (during the years 1912–19, 1923–29 and 1931–33). He was a colorful character, as *The Arizona Republican* commented in a 1911 editorial: "Two circuses are in town today, Ringling Brothers and G.W.P. Hunt. Both are complete with side shows." In 1920 Hunt took time out from his busy schedule to serve as the American Consul to Siam (Thailand).

Arizonans fondly called Hunt "the Old Roman," but his passion was Egyptology. He is buried (along with his wife and their dog) beneath a big, white Egyptian-style pyramid, complete with hieroglyphics, just outside the Phoenix Zoo.

DID YOU KNOW?

Famed dancer and actress Ann Miller (whose maternal grand-mother was Cherokee) lived in Sedona and believed herself to have been, in a former life, Hatshepsut, Queen of Egypt, who reigned from 1479 to 1458 BC.

Most Important Person

In 2002, on the occasion of Arizona's 90th year of statehood, Carl Trumbull Hayden was voted the most important person in Arizona's history. After serving in various local political offices—Tempe Town Council, Maricopa County Treasurer, Maricopa County Sheriff—he went to Washington, DC, and today he holds the national record for longest service in the U.S. Congress: 57 years. A Democrat, he was a Representative from 1912 to 1927 (eight terms) and a Senator from 1927 to 1969 (seven terms). To put that in perspective, Hayden was in Washington, representing Arizona, through World War I, the Roaring Twenties, Prohibition, the Wall Street Crash, the Dust Bowl, the Great Depression, World War II, the Korean War and the War in Vietnam.

President John F. Kennedy said of Carl Hayden, "Every federal program which has contributed to the development of the West—irrigation, power, reclamation—bears his mark, and the great federal highway program which binds this country together, which permits Arizona to be competitive east and west, north and south, this in large measure is his creation."

But Hayden didn't merely help only his own state. *The Los Angeles Times* wrote in 1971 that "He has assisted so many projects for so many senators that when old Carl wants something for his beloved Arizona, his fellow senators fall all over themselves giving him a hand. They'd probably vote landlocked Arizona a navy if he asked for it." Carl Hayden was born on October 2, 1877—the first white child ever born in Tempe—and died in 1972, just before his 95th birthday.

Pork Lite

In "pork spending" (government spending that benefits constituents of a politician in return for their political support), Arizona ranks dead last in the nation. In 2008, Arizona, the second fastest growing state in the nation, received $18.70 per capita in federal earmarks. In comparison, Alaska (with roughly a tenth of Arizona's population) received $506.34 per capita, the highest in the nation—making Alaska, the state with the Big Dipper on its flag, the biggest dipper of federal pork.

THE ARTS AND MUSEUMS

The West's Most Eastern Western Town

Scottsdale calls itself "the West's Most Western Town," but it has a far larger art scene than any eastern city except New York. With more than 200 art galleries, thousands of resident painters and sculptors, hundreds of world-class private collections, multiple fine-art museums and the prestigious Scottsdale Artists' School, to which the top artists fly from all over the world to teach week-long classes, Scottsdale is hardly the quintessential cow-town. Paloma Picasso, Pablo's daughter, once owned an art gallery in Scottsdale. In the 1980s and '90s, the world's largest-circulation newspaper, *Art-Talk,* was published in Scottsdale, which today is the home of America's premiere art magazine, *American Art Collector.*

A Multitude of Museums

Arizona has 122 museums, including the Titan Missile Museum in Sahuarita, the Hall of Flame Museum of Firefighting in Phoenix, the McElhaney Museum of wagons and buggies in Wellton (29 miles east of Yuma) and the Rex Allen Museum in Willcox. Rex Allen is known as "The Arizona Cowboy," but he was an actor, songwriter and singer—and he provided the narration for *Charlotte's Web,* the 1973 animated film. He has a star on the Hollywood Walk of Fame. He was born in Mud Springs Canyon, near Willcox.

DID YOU  KNOW?

The director of Flagstaff's Museum of Northern Arizona was Edward Bridge Danson Jr., father of Ted Danson, star of the TV sitcom *Cheers* (1982–93).

Have You Heard of the Heard?

Arizona's finest and most popular museum (250,000 visitors per year) is the Heard Museum of Native Cultures and Art. Founded in downtown Phoenix in 1929 by Dwight B. and Maie Bartlett Heard to house their personal collection, the Heard now has more than 40,000 artifacts, including Barry Goldwater's collection of 437 historic kachina dolls.

AMAZING ARIZONA Arizona's oldest cultural institution is the Arizona Historical Society (AHS), which was founded by the Territorial legislature on November 7, 1864. There are now AHS museums in Flagstaff, Tempe, Tucson and Yuma.

The Performing Arts

The Tucson Symphony Orchestra is the oldest professional performing arts organization in Arizona—its first performance took place on January 13, 1929, in the Tucson High School Auditorium. Arizona's longest continuously performing choral organization, also begun in 1929, is the Orpheus Male Chorus of Phoenix, which has performed concerts throughout the United States and in 14 foreign countries, including Ireland.

The Emerald Isle's music is now here too, thanks to the Arizona Irish Music Society. You're more interested in jazz? It's robustly alive and well here, thanks to Jazz in AZ, which was founded in 1977. (Jazz great Charles Mingus, 1922–79, was born in Nogales, Arizona.) Interested in square dancing? Join one of the Grand Canyon Square Dance Association's numerous clubs. You'd rather watch more classical dances? Arizona Opera began in Tucson in 1971 and since 1975 has also been performing in Phoenix, and in 1986 the Phoenix Ballet, Ballet West Arizona and the Arizona Dance Theater all were combined to form Ballet Arizona.

ARCHITECTURE

Architects' Mecca at the End of the World

Taliesin was Frank Lloyd Wright's home in Wisconsin. Wanting also a warmer home, he came to Arizona and found an area so remote and sparsely populated that he telegraphed friends back East that he had found the perfect site "at the end of the world." Opened in 1937, Taliesin West, Wright's western home, was also a studio and school for great architects, including Wright's apprentice, William Wesley Peters, who married Joseph Stalin's daughter, Svetlana. Some of Wright's greatest buildings were designed in his Arizona studio, including the Guggenheim Museum in New York. Taliesin West is open to the public but is hardly at the end of the world anymore—it's a 20-minute drive from downtown Scottsdale.

DID YOU  KNOW?

One of the students who came to Scottsdale to attend Taliesin West was Antonio Rudolfo Oaxaca Quinn, from the Mexican state of Chihuahua. Frank Lloyd Wright himself suggested to the young man that he should become an actor instead of an architect. Antonio did so, and as Anthony Quinn he became world-famous for his title role in *Zorba the Greek* (1964).

For Iraq—Not

The crown architectural jewel on the Tempe campus of Arizona State University (ASU) was originally intended to be an opera house in Baghdad. Frank Lloyd Wright's last public commission, the big salmon-colored structure (300 feet long, 250 feet wide and 80 feet high, with twin 200-foot "flying buttress" walkways) with its "perfect acoustics" is Arizona's premiere venue for the performing arts. Named after Wright's friend, ASU President Grady Gammage, Gammage Auditorium opened in 1964 with Eugene Ormandy leading the Philadelphia Orchestra. The opera house that Iraq lost has been on the U.S. National Register of Historic Places since 1985.

The State Capitol

Virginia architect James Riely Gordon (1863–1937) designed the building, basing his plan on a failed proposal for the Mississippi State Capitol. The Arizona State Capitol opened in 1901, its dominant feature the copper dome topped by the white wind vane. The 15 tons of copper used for the dome is equivalent to 4.8 million pennies, and the wind vane (made of zinc) is called Winged Victory. The original capitol building is now a museum, the work of state government being conducted in the much larger complex of buildings directly behind it.

MEDIA

Arizona's Mightiest Magazine

Two magazines premiered in 1925: *The New Yorker,* today the ultimate publication for East Coast refinement; and an engineering journal published by the Arizona Highway Department to report on road construction and maintenance in the state, *Arizona Highways,* today the ultimate publication for the wonder and majesty of the West. *The New Yorker* has always been famous for its cartoons; *Arizona Highways* has been famous for its photographs ever since it ran photos taken by the great Ansel Adams. Today *Arizona Highways* has subscribers in more than 100 countries and in all 50 states nationwide—and it's still published by the Arizona Department of Transportation.

Arizona Newspapers

Arizona's first newspaper was *The Weekly Arizonan,* published in Tubac, its first issue appearing on March 3, 1859. The oldest continuously published newspaper in Arizona is *The Tucson Citizen,* which began on October 15, 1870—coincidentally the same day that General Robert E. Lee was buried in Lexington, Virginia. Tucson's other major newspaper today, *The Arizona Daily Star,* began publication in 1879. A decade later, Territorial Governor Lewis Wolfley (Republican, 1889–90) decided that existing Arizona newspapers were biased. So he and his Attorney General, Clark Churchill, started their own newspaper, *The Arizona Republican,* which published its first edition on May 19, 1890. By 1915, this paper had the largest circulation in the state. On November 11, 1930, it was renamed *The Arizona Republic,* and the following week it purchased *The Phoenix Evening Gazette* and *The Arizona Weekly.* Those papers later became *The Phoenix Gazette* and *The Arizona Business Gazette.*

Radio

Arizona Governor John Howard Pyle definitely understood the power of the media—from 1930 to 1951, he was program director at KFAD Radio. Established in June 1922, KFAD was Arizona's first radio station. That was right at the beginning of sports broadcasting. The first-ever radio broadcast of a sports event occurred on July 2, 1921 (the Jack "Manassa Mauler" Dempsey v. Georges "Orchid Man" Carpentier prizefight), and a month later, on August 5, 1921, Americans heard the first broadcast of a baseball game (Pittsburgh Pirates v. Philadelphia Phillies).

In 1929 KFAD was purchased by *The Arizona Republic* newspaper, and in 1930 the call letters were changed to KTAR, an acronym for "Keep Taking the *Arizona Republic*." From 1939 to 1975, KTAR was the flagship of the Arizona Broadcasting System, which had affiliate stations in Tucson, Prescott, Globe and Yuma.

DID YOU KNOW?

The first Arizona governor born in the 20th century, John Howard Pyle (1906–87) took time off from his radio job to serve as a war correspondent and was aboard the USS *Missouri* in Tokyo Harbor to record the Japanese surrender ceremony.

TV Trivia

Premiering on December 4, 1949, KPHO (Channel 5) was Arizona's first TV station. KPNX (Channel 12), founded in 1953, is the only major English-language commercial TV station in Phoenix to never have changed its primary affiliation.

Paving the Way to *Sesame Street*

Four generations of Arizona children watched *The Wallace and Ladmo Show*, the longest-running daily children's television show in history. Airing on KPHO-TV in Phoenix, the show ran for 36 years, from April 3, 1954, to December 29, 1989. Bill Thompson was the Wallace character, and Ladimir Kwiatkowski was Ladmo. Phoenix native Joan Ganz Cooney watched Wallace and Ladmo, then went on to create and produce her own, far more famous, children's TV show, with Big Bird, Bert and Ernie, Oscar the Grouch and Cookie Monster: *Sesame Street*. Cooney was the co-founder of the Children's Television Workshop. In 1995 she was awarded the Presidential Medal of Freedom.

ENTERTAINMENT

When Arizona became a state, in 1912, virtually all entertainment in America was "live"—to experience it, you had to be there in person. There was no radio at all (until the first broadcast in America: December 24, 1906), no television (until the first regularly scheduled TV service: July 2, 1928), and movies were just getting started. The first movie shot in Hollywood (In Old California) *was released on March 10, 1910. On October 6, 1927,* The Jazz Singer *premiered, marking the end of the silent film era.*

Arizona Music & Entertainment Hall of Fame

This institution, coordinated from Scottsdale, recognizes and honors the contributions of musicians, entertainers and individuals who have had a significant impact on the evolution and development of Arizona's musical and entertainment culture. Some of the most famous Hall of Famers include:

Rex Allen, actor and singer and the voice of more than 150 Disney cartoon characters

Jana Bommersbach, columnist and author

Al Casey, guitarist

Glen Campbell, singer

Sanford Clark, guitarist and songwriter

Jessi Colter, singer

Mike Condello, musician

William Edward Compton, radio DJ

Alice Cooper, singer

Dyke & The Blazers, singers

Dwight Harkins, movie theater pioneer

Herndon Family & Handlebar J, entertainers

Waylon Jennings, singer

Lew King, entertainer named "Mr. Arizona" in 1974

Michael Lacey, publisher

Wallace & Ladmo, children's TV pioneers

Charles Lewis, musician

Pat McMahon, talk-show host

Jack Miller, studio engineer

R. Carlos Nakai, musician
(Native American flute)

Wayne Newton, singer

Stevie Nicks, singer

Buck Owens, singer

Floyd Ramsey, record store
pioneer

Jerry Riopelle, singer

Marty Robbins, singer

Linda Ronstadt, singer

Fritz Scholder, painter

Steven Spielberg, director

Dwight Tindle, radio pioneer

The Tubes, entertainers

Dee Dee Wood, dancer and
choreographer

Danny Zelisko, music
promoter

A Few Other Arizona Entertainers

☛ Hollywood supporting actress Christine McIntyre, who
starred in 22 feature films (including all *The Three Stooges*
movies from 1944 to 1950), was born in Nogales, Arizona.

☛ Guitarist, singer and farm labor activist Lalo Guerrero, who
in 1980 was named a National Folk Treasure by the
Smithsonian Institution, was born in Tucson.

☛ Also born in the Old Pueblo (Tucson) was singer and musician Ted Ramirez, who in 2001 was proclaimed by the mayor
and city council "Tucson's Official Troubadour." Founder of
the Santa Cruz River Band and creator and host of "Sounds
of Arizona" (a statewide radio program that features
Southwestern folk music), Ramirez has a remarkable pedigree
in this state where native-born people are becoming rarer: he
is an eighth-generation Arizonan, a direct descendant of a
Tubac Presidio captain of the Army of Spain. The Arizona
Culture Keeper Award in 2004 was presented to Ted
Ramirez.

DID YOU  KNOW?

Where there is music, there was first music education. Arizona's first public school music teacher was Mary Ethelyn Ruffner, who arrived in Phoenix in 1867.

Almost the Mecca of Movies
Released in 1903, the first Western film, *The Great Train Robbery*, thrilled audiences with its scenes from the "Wild West," which had been shot in the wilds of New Jersey and in Thomas Edison's studio. Amazed and pleased by the public reaction to that 12-minute film, Edison and his partners sent a scouting party west to find an authentic locale for additional Western movies. Their first choice was Flagstaff, Arizona. But after a freak blizzard they continued westward, finally settling on a little California town called Hollywood.

Cameras, Action!

Prescott, Arizona, was making movies before Hollywood was. The first feature film made in Hollywood, in 1914, was *The Squaw Man,* directed by Cecil B. DeMille. But Prescott first attracted the movie industry in 1912, and major studios still film there today. The movie *Junior Bonner,* starring Steve McQueen (1971), was filmed at The Palace, Prescott's oldest saloon and today Arizona's oldest restaurant.

Cameras, Action, State!

On February 14, 1912, when President William H. Taft signed the proclamation making Arizona the 48th state, cameras rolled, and that signing was the first presidential ceremony ever to be recorded by movie cameras.

Some Films Shot Partially or Wholly in Arizona

3:10 to Yuma

A Kiss Before Dying

A Star Is Born

Alice Doesn't Live Here Anymore

Anastasia

Back to the Future

Beau Geste

Bill & Ted's Excellent Adventure

Cannonball Run

Can't Buy Me Love

Casablanca

Clear and Present Danger

Death Wish

Easy Rider

Electra Glide in Blue

Exorcist II: The Heretic

The Flight of the Phoenix

Forrest Gump

The Greatest Story Ever Told

The Grifters

Gunfight at the O.K. Corral

How the West Was Won

The Karate Kid

Lilies of the Field

National Lampoon's Vacation

Near Dark

The Nutty Professor

Planet of the Apes

Psycho

The Quick and the Dead

Raising Arizona

Rambo III

Revenge of the Nerds

The Scorpion King

The Shawshank Redemption

Song of the South

Spaceballs

Star Wars, Episode VI: Return of the Jedi

Stargate

Starman

Thelma & Louise

¡Three Amigos!

Universal Soldier

Waiting to Exhale

The War of the Worlds

Wayne's World

Young Guns II

AMAZING ARIZONA When he opened the State Theater in Tempe in 1933, Dwight Harkins, 18, was the youngest movie theater operator in the world. Still owned by the Harkins family, and today headquartered in Scottsdale, Harkins Theaters is the premiere entertainment company in the Southwest, with more than 400 screens throughout Arizona and in California, Texas and Oklahoma.

Spielberg Started Here

As a young teen, Steven Spielberg shot his first 8-mm "adventure" movie in a Scottsdale restaurant.

Arizona in *Oklahoma!*

Oklahoma!, the first musical by Rodgers and Hammerstein, opened on Broadway in 1943. The 1955 movie version's opening sequence, "Oh, what a beautiful mornin'," was filmed south of Tucson, in Amado (Santa Cruz County). Much of the rest of that film was shot in Nogales, which was chosen because it looked more like turn-of-the-century Oklahoma than anywhere in Oklahoma did in 1955. By order of Arizona Governor John Howard Pyle, Nogales was made an honorary part of the State of Oklahoma for the duration of the film shoot.

ARIZONA AND OTHER WORLDS

A Century of Astronomy

Arizona has been a world leader in astronomy for exactly one century, since a Flagstaff astronomer named Percival Lowell published *Mars as the Abode of Life* in 1908. He was the founder of the Lowell Observatory west of Flagstaff, and his initials were intentionally memorialized in "PLuto," the "planet" discovered through the telescope there. Lowell died in 1916, long before Clyde Tombaugh found Pluto in 1930. Lowell was obsessed with proving that Mars had intelligent life. His obsession inspired H.G. Wells to write *War of the Worlds.* Lowell studied the "canals" on Mars for 15 years before publishing his book. Because of that 1908 book, many people today insist that Mars once had intelligent life forms—and NASA is spending billions of dollars trying to find out whether Flagstaff's Percival Lowell was right.

Is There Really Life Out There?

University of Arizona astrobiologist Margaret Turnbull recently identified a star named "37 Geminorum" as the star most likely to have life in its vicinity. The star is a yellow-white main sequence dwarf that is 56.3 light years from us. A transmission named the "Teen Age Message" was sent to 37 Geminorum on September 3, 2001, and will arrive at the star in December 2057. Turnbull, who received her PhD in Astronomy at the University of Arizona, was named a "Genius" by CNN in 2007 for her work cataloging stars most likely to develop planets that could support life and intelligent civilizations. The asteroid "7863 Turnbull" was named in her honor.

The *Really* Wide Open Spaces

For watching outer space, Arizona has 11 observatories, three related research organizations and 22 astronomy clubs. In 2006, astronomy, planetary and space sciences had a $252-million impact on Arizona's economy, generated more than 3300 jobs and welcomed 201,000 visitors (7000 professionals, 194,000 general public). One Arizona observatory, Kitt Peak, with 23 telescopes, is the largest and most diverse gathering of major astronomical instruments in the world—including the McMath-Pierce Solar Telescope, the largest solar telescope on earth.

Observatories in or Near Flagstaff

Astronomical Adventures Observatory

Braeside Observatory

Lowell Observatory

Northern Arizona University Atmospheric Research Observatory

U.S. Naval Observatory

Observatories in or Near Tucson
Grasslands Observatory

Kitt Peak National Observatory

MMT (Multiple-Mirror Telescope) Observatory

National Optical Astronomy Observatories

Sabino Canyon Observatory

Steward Observatory

Vega-Bray Observatory

Observatories in or Near Safford (Graham County)
Discovery Park Astronomical Society

Governor Aker Observatory

Mount Graham International Observatory

Observatory in Amado (Santa Cruz County)
Fred Lawrence Whipple Observatory (Mount Hopkins)

The Vatican in Arizona

Founded in Rome in 1774, the Vatican Observatory is one of the oldest astronomical research institutions in the world. Today it has a branch in Arizona: the Vatican Observatory Research Group, hosted by the Steward Observatory at the University of Arizona in Tucson. The Vatican Observatory Research Group operates the 1.8-m. Alice P. Lennon Telescope with its Thomas J. Bannan Astrophysics Facility, known together as the Vatican Advanced Technology Telescope (VATT), at the Mount Graham International Observatory (MGIO) in Safford, in southeastern Arizona.

Join the Club

The state's numerous astronomy clubs include the Astronomers of Verde Valley, 24 members (Cottonwood); the Astronomy Club of Sun City West, 120 members; and the East Valley Astronomy Club, 235 members (Mesa).

UFOs?

Fire in the Sky, a 1993 movie starring D.B. Sweeney and James Garner, is all about the alleged abduction of Travis Walton by a UFO in Arizona's Apache-Sitgreaves National Forests in 1975. That was merely one of countless unexplained celestial phenomena reported by ufologists in Arizona, where sightings of space aliens are almost as common as sightings of illegal aliens. Many UFO sightings are reported from the area around Sedona, which is also world-famous for its red rocks and its New Age beliefs in such things as psychic vortices at Schnebly Hills, Airport Mesa, Bell Rock, Cathedral Rock and Boynton Canyon.

Space Center Designed by Arizona Kids

Fifth- and sixth-grade students helped to design the Challenger Space Center, and then for four years helped various interested groups to raise $3.5 million to build it in Peoria, just west of Phoenix. Now with a staff of 150 (adults), the center is affiliated with the Smithsonian Institution, and Diane McCarthy, president of the Arizona State University Alumni Association, recently said, "Having the Challenger Space Center as a Smithsonian affiliate is an enormous advantage to the West Valley. This gives us an opportunity to market and highlight space as only the Smithsonian can."

Since the center's grand opening on July 23, 2000, more than 100,000 visitors—65,000 of them school children—have experienced simulated space missions, space camps, lectures, classes, stargazing nights and special programs like "Rendezvous With a Comet."

Arizona Science Center

Located in downtown Phoenix, the Arizona Science Center opened in 1984—and that first year had 87,000 visitors. It has an IMAX theater with seating for 285 and a multi-media Dorrance Planetarium with seating for 200 beneath one of the largest domes in the West. The center also has more than 300 interactive exhibits organized into galleries that explore human physiology, physical forces, transportation, geology, computers and applied sciences.

Dating Capital of the World—for Trees

Tree-ring dating is a scientific discipline, called "dendrochronology," and was founded at the University of Arizona, in Tucson, by A.E. Douglass. An astronomer, Douglass discovered that solar activity correlated with tree rings. Announcing his discovery in the December 1929 issue of *National Geographic,* he showed that a log he collected in Show Low, Arizona, could be accurately and reliably dated back to 1237 AD.

Patents Aplenty

An estimated 73 percent of all patents granted in the United States are attributable to scientific research initially funded by taxpayers through the federal government, especially university research operations. In 2007 in Arizona, 204 contractors earned $1.14 billion in federal research and development contract expenditures. The University of Arizona is consistently ranked among the top 20 public research universities in the United States.

High-Tech Arizona

☛ Arizona is the country's third biggest semiconductor manufacturing state by employment.

☛ The state employs 36,700 semiconductor-manufacturing workers, behind only California and Texas.

☛ Arizona ranks 19th in industrial electronics manufacturing employment (with 4700 jobs) and 20th in electronics components and accessories employment (with 6900 jobs).

☛ Arizona has a high-tech payroll of $5.2 billion.

☛ High-tech exports total $6.2 billion.

☛ The state has 92,375 high-tech workers.

☛ High-tech firms employ 52 of every 1000 private sector workers in Arizona.

☛ High-tech workers earn an average wage that is 94 percent more than the average private sector wage.

☛ Arizona has more than 3000 high-tech establishments.

The Widow-Makers

State-of-the-art technology has not always been beneficial. Early Arizona miners practiced dry drilling with pneumatic drills that were called "widow-makers"—they created so much dust that the operators frequently died of silicosis after only a year or two of work. Dry drilling was finally outlawed in 1968.

AMAZING ARIZONA TASER International, Inc., developer, manufacturer and distributor of the electroshock device, was founded in Scottsdale, Arizona, in 1993—but its name honors a boy who appeared in 1910. The publication that year of *Tom Swift and His Motor Cycle,* a juvenile adventure book, generated the kind of nationwide excitement and devotion never seen again until the *Harry Potter* series. A new *Tom Swift* title was released roughly once each year for an amazing 31 years—all together, 40 different books starring the teenager who lived in upstate New York and above all loved speed (hence his name: Swift).

The *Tom Swift* series was so wildly popular and lasted so long because each book in the series focused on whatever was newest and most exciting in the world of technology. The second book in the series was about Tom and his "motor boat," the third was about him and his "airship," the fourth was about Tom and his "submarine boat." The eleventh book, *Tom Swift and His Electric Rifle*, inspired the name of the law enforcement tool now used all over the world: Tom A. Swift's Electric Rifle— TASER.

ROGUES AND HEROES

The Lady Outlaw People Loved

The first woman ever to rob a stagecoach robbed it in Arizona. A French Canadian named Pearl Hart was born in Lindsey, near Toronto, in 1870. She moved to Phoenix in 1892, and on May 29, 1899, robbed the stagecoach at Cane Spring in the Dripping Springs Mountains, just south of the Pinals. Hart was caught six days later and placed in the Florence Jail, but was subsequently moved to the Pima County Jail in Tucson. She was an instant media sensation, the public mostly taking her side after she declared that, as a woman, she refused to consent to be tried by any law made solely by men. On October 12 she escaped and fled to New Mexico, where she was eventually recaptured. Arizona Territorial Governor Alexander Brodie pardoned her on December 19, 1902. Pearl Hart moved to Dripping Springs, Arizona, and died in 1956, and her only "crime" during the last 50 years of her life was said to have been that she was fond of cigars.

Larger-Than-Life Characters

Maricopa County Sheriff Joe Arpaio is the most famous sheriff in North America partly because he's Joe Arpaio and partly because, in Arizona, both lawmen and criminals have always nudged up to legendary status. Billy the Kid shot and killed his first man in a saloon in Camp Grant. Jack Swilling was a scam artist, a drug addict, a stagecoach robber, a murderer of as many as 12 men and an army deserter—and, in 1870, he founded the city of Phoenix. In Tombstone, Wyatt Earp was the Joe Arpaio of his day. In 1934, John Dillinger said, "Well, I'll be damned," when he was captured in Tucson.

More Recent Spectacular Crimes

☛ A number of the 9/11 terrorists lived and trained in Arizona.

☛ Bob Crane (star of TV's *Hogan's Heroes*) was murdered in Scottsdale in 1978.

☛ *Arizona Republic* reporter Don Bolles, working on an organized-crime story, was murdered by a car bomb in Phoenix in 1976.

☛ Throughout the United States today, law enforcement is restricted as the result of a Phoenix case in 1963. Ernesto Miranda (1941–76) was arrested on suspicion of a kidnap/rape and convicted solely on the basis of his own confession. Because he had not been informed of his rights and was not given access to an attorney, his appeal made it all the way to the U.S. Supreme Court and resulted in "the Miranda warning."

☛ Territorial Arizona sent all its worst criminals to Yuma. For 33 years (1876–1909), the Yuma prison housed 29 female convicts, including Pearl Hart, and 3040 men, one of them "Buckskin" Frank Leslie, who confessed to killing 14 men. You can tour the Yuma Territorial Prison State Park today and watch events that include "The Gathering of the Gunfighters" (second weekend in January) and "Haunted Tours" (last Saturday in October).

Modern Prisons All Over

Arizona State prisons, prison complexes and correctional facilities today are located in Douglas, Eyman, Florence (two), Holbrook, Lewis, Marana, Perryville, Phoenix, Safford, Tucson, Winslow and (a new one) Yuma. The Yuma convicts who built the state prison in Florence that replaced the Territorial one lived in tents during the construction—a 1908 version of Sheriff Joe's nationally known "Tent City."

Tent City

Maricopa County Sheriff Joe Arpaio has been called "America's Toughest Sheriff" for his insistence that convicted criminals should not be treated like honored guests of the state. To handle the overcrowding problem without county taxpayers having to pay $70 million for a new jail, Sheriff Joe instituted "Tent City," housing thousands of convicts in hundreds of tents inside a guarded fence. Other innovations that have outraged prison activists and delighted the general public include restricting prisoner access to television and pornography, requiring male inmates to wear pink underwear, serving inmates green (oxidized) bologna sandwiches, bringing back chain gangs and organizing a permanent posse—whose vehicles include a black tank.

Deadly Gunfighters—Not

The reputations of all the Old West's famous gunfighters are wildly exaggerated, and the actual deadliest gunfighters were all men that few people have ever heard of, like Jim Miller and Tom Horn. Wyatt Earp's total confirmed kills during formal gunfights: 0. The Sundance Kid: 0. Jesse James, Bat Masterson and Johnny Ringo: one each. Doc Holliday: two. Billy the Kid: four. Jim Miller: 12. Tom Horn: 20. Horn's total doesn't include the men he killed legally—he took a break from his career as a killer for hire to join the army and go to Cuba to kill Spaniards. After the Spanish American War he returned to his career as a hired killer, and at age 43, in Wyoming, was lynched for a killing that he actually didn't commit. Steve McQueen starred as the should-be-more-famous gunfighter in *Tom Horn* (1980).

Hohokam Genocide

Virtually overnight, almost all of Arizona's most accomplished people vanished. The year was around 1450 AD, the people were the Hohokam, and over the preceding centuries they had built, by hand, the largest and most sophisticated irrigation system in the world. Before the builders disappeared, more than 1000 miles of canals were irrigating 100,000 acres in central Arizona—and they were built so well that a number of those ancient canals are still carrying water through Metro Phoenix. But then one day the Hohokam's capital city, Snaketown, and all the smaller towns, had suddenly become ghost towns. What happened? The Aztecs arrived. From their capital, Tenochtitlan, present-day Mexico City, they periodically sent out armies to collect human victims to sacrifice to the sun.

The sun was insatiable: during special Aztec festivals, people were sacrificed at the rate of one every 15 seconds, nonstop from dawn to sunset. All neighboring tribes were rapidly wiped out, and the Aztecs had to search ever farther afield to find victims. The Aztec army that kidnapped the Hohokam people and took them south to feed the sun missed a few, and those survivors were the ancestors of the modern-day Tohono O'odham and Akimel Nations, also known as the Papago and the Pima.

Other Various Crimes

☛ According to the FBI Crime Index, Arizona ranks second in the nation for larceny-theft, fourth for burglary, 13th in overall violent crime, 17th for aggravated assault and 24th for rape.

☛ Vice. Joseph H. Kibbey, the next to last Territorial Governor (1905–09) tried to outlaw of gambling, restrict liquor and tobacco and prohibit prostitution. In 1907 a state law drove extensive gambling and "hostesses" from bars throughout Arizona, and most saloons were closed during World War I.

- Land Fraud. "The Baron of Arizona," a forger named James Addison Reavis, masterminded the Peralta Grant Scandal, one of the greatest land fraud schemes in American history. By forging documents in Old Spanish, he came close to getting title to 18,750 square miles of land in Central Arizona—including the entire Superstition Mountains Wilderness Area (supposed site of the legendary Lost Dutchman Gold Mine). When a Florence journalist named Thomas F. Weedin proved that the documents' paper and ink were far too recent to date from Colonial Spain, Reavis was arrested. He was tried on June 27, 1896, and sentenced to two years in prison.

- Criminal Cockroaches! Phoenix ranks second in the nation for fast food health violations. Past violations include a complaint against a Phoenix McDonald's, in which a customer alleged that her child found two roaches in her pancakes.

☛ Cattle Rustling. After 1870, Arizona law required that all brands be burned on leather and registered with the Territorial brand inspector.

☛ Murder. According to the FBI Crime Index, Arizona ranks number five in the nation for murder. The most famous was the case of Winnie Ruth Judd, a 25-year-old medical secretary in Phoenix who shot and killed her two roommates in 1931. One of the bodies was stuffed into one shipping trunk and the other body was hacked into pieces to fit into another, both trunks to be sent by train to Los Angeles. The case of "The Trunk Murderess" received worldwide attention, with newspapers calling Judd the "Arizona Tigress," "Tiger Woman," "Wolf Woman" and the "Blonde Butcher." She was sentenced to be hanged on February 17, 1933, but the death sentence was repealed and she was sent to the Arizona State Hospital, from where she escaped seven times. She died in 1998, at age 93.

Psycho!

Speaking of shocking murders, the greatest horror movie of all time—number one on the American Film Institute's list of the 100 Best Thrillers ever made—is Alfred Hitchcock's *Psycho* (1960), which was shot partly in Phoenix. The film was based on a 1959 novel of the same name in which the heroine is Mary Crane. Because an actual Mary Crane lived in Phoenix at the time of the shooting, Hitchcock changed his Phoenix heroine's name to Marion Crane (played by Janet Leigh).

There's Two of Me!

Arizona leads the nation in identity theft. In 2006, one in six adults had had their identities stolen in the preceding five years, about twice the national rate, according to *The New York Times* (May 30, 2006). In 2007, a total of 293,500 Arizonans were victimized—a 55 percent increase from 2002. The problem is compounded by illegal aliens who enter Arizona and get fake identities.

The Human Flood

The biggest crime problem in Arizona today is that of illegal residence following illegal border crossing at numerous points along Arizona's 389-mile border with Mexico. In the Tucson sector of the border alone, approximately 1000 illegal-entry aliens are arrested every day. The problem is compounded by activists who view heritage and intentions as more relevant than illegality, arguing that Mexicans who want to come here "for a better life" should be allowed to do so. That argument is flatly rejected by those who say that regardless of intention or fine Hispanic heritage, the law is the law, and, moreover, the border-crossers' quest for a better life is resulting in a worse life for residents.

The Federation for American Immigration Reform (FAIR) estimated in 2007 that Arizona's illegal alien population was 475,000 people, and that the illegal immigrant population costs the state's taxpayers about $1.3 billion per year for education, medical care and incarceration—which works out to $3.56 million of tax money every 24 hours. In Tucson, which has one of the busiest federal courthouses in the country, approximately 100 illegal aliens are charged and processed through the federal court system every day. Many who are deported simply turn around and slip back into Arizona.

Famous Lawbreakers

☛ Sonny Barger, founder of the Hells Angels, was imprisoned in Florence for having tried to blow up another motorcycle gang's clubhouse.

☛ Bomber Timothy McVeigh lived in Kingman, and while there made his plans to blow up the federal building in Oklahoma City.

☛ In 1991, actor Johnny Depp was pulled over for speeding near Tucson.

☛ Celebrities arrested in Arizona include singer Diane Ross; Axl Rose, front man for Guns 'N Roses; and Jim Morrison of The Doors.

On the Run

The Arizona Republic estimated on April 27, 2008, that there were approximately one million fugitives in the United States, including 59,000 felony warrants in Arizona—42,000 in Maricopa County alone—for people wanted on charges ranging from identity theft to murder.

Criminal Kids

For crimes committed by people 18 or younger, the city of Gilbert had Maricopa County's highest number of arrests in 2007:

☛ DUI and liquor laws—461 arrests

☛ Curfew—455 arrests

☛ Theft and burglary—248 arrests

☛ Runaway—212 arrests

☛ Drug possession—170 arrests

Shannon's Law

Before July 1, 2000, it was a mere misdemeanor to randomly discharge a firearm into the air in Phoenix. That used to happen a lot—on New Year's Eve 1999, Phoenix police received 994 "shots fired" calls. But one of those bullets that night came back down and killed 14-year-old Shannon Smith. Outrage over her death led to the passage of "Shannon's Law," making it a felony to randomly shoot a gun into the air. More than 1300 mourners showed up for Shannon's funeral, and her friends had a school memorial to her made out of metal from melted-down confiscated guns.

Marijuana

On January 17, 2008, U.S. Customs and Border Protection officers in San Luis intercepted the largest amount of marijuana ever seized in Arizona: 3043 pounds, worth just under $5 million. In comparison, the largest amount of marijuana ever seized by the RCMP in Labrador was 18 pounds, worth $160,000 (in 2007). Most marijuana is smuggled in from Mexico, but Arizonans also grow their own: five marijuana gardens were found in Tonto National Forest and one in Coconino National Forest.

Illegal Drugs

In 2004 in the Tucson area alone, Drug Enforcement Administration (DEA) agents seized:

marijuana	689,305 pounds
cocaine	7887 pounds
meth	1149 pounds
heroin	196 pounds

In the same area that year, DEA agents also confiscated 882 Ecstasy tablets and raided 122 meth labs. An Arizona Youth Survey in 2006 found that 4.3 percent of Arizona children aged 13–17 had tried methamphetamine. According to Maricopa County Attorney Andrew Thomas, Arizona in 2005 had a higher instance of meth users than any other state.

AMAZING ARIZONA Throughout the United States and Canada today, and elsewhere in the world, the wishes of children with life-threatening medical conditions are granted, thanks to an act of kindness nearly 30 years ago by patrol officer Ron Cox of the Arizona Department of Public Safety (DPS). When Cox heard that a seven-year-old Phoenix boy who was dying of leukemia had always dreamed of growing up to be a police officer, he quickly got DPS approval to make the little boy's dream come true. On April 29, 1980, Chris Greicius (pronounced "gracious") became the first and only Honorary State Trooper in DPS history. Chris received a tour of Phoenix in a police helicopter, which then flew him to headquarters for a meeting with DPS command staff.

Chris told Arizona's top law-enforcement brass about his earlier law-enforcement "career" of driving around his neighborhood on his battery-powered three-wheel motorcycle and writing "tickets" to put on windshields. So a DPS motorcycle proficiency test was set up for the boy. Employees at a local company, John's Uniforms, stayed up all night custom-tailoring a patrolman uniform for him, and his fellow patrol officers found a miniature "Smokey the Bear" campaign hat for him to wear. On May 1, they held the proficiency test, and Chris, on his own battery-operated motorcycle, passed easily, earning the department's wings badge to pin on his uniform. The next day, May 2, 1980, Chris died. Word spread of his passing, and the result was the Make-a-Wish Foundation, which was established in 1981, and the Canadian branch, established in 1983.

LET THE GAMES BEGIN

Sports Galore

Arizona offers year-round golf, tennis, horseback riding, bicycle riding, hiking, hunting and fishing. Spectator sports include all the "big" ones—basketball, football, baseball, ice hockey—plus Indy and sprint car racing, arena football, indoor soccer, roller hockey and thoroughbred and greyhound racing. College fans can enjoy intercollegiate athletics at all three major state universities, in Tempe, Tucson and Flagstaff.

It isn't just a great place to play, but also a great place to live—current or former Arizona residents include boxer Muhammad Ali (Paradise Valley), home-run king Barry Bonds (he graduated from Arizona State University and lived in Phoenix), baseball great Joe Garagiola (Phoenix) and Olympic gymnast Olga Korbut (Scottsdale).

Prehistoric Basketball

The earliest professional sport in Arizona was basketball, played in the Metro Phoenix area 1000 years ago. Called *tlachtli,* basketball was the most popular of all sports among the Hohokam of Arizona as well as the Aztecs and the Maya. The playing area was rectangular, and the two teams tried to bounce the hollow rubber ball through a stone hoop that was positioned vertically rather than horizontally. When Europeans arrived in the New World, their first sight of rubber was one of those *tlachtli* balls. From Arizona south to the Yucatan, the game was wildly popular, and sports betting was rampant—men wagered gold, jewelry, feathered cloaks, cornfields and sometimes their own wives and children, on the outcome of games—and the ball courts were always packed.

Snaketown, the Hohokams' main city, near present-day Chandler, had two ball courts. Another big one was built near "the Stack" in Phoenix, the four-level interchange of the Papago Freeway (I-10) and the Black Canyon Freeway (I-17)—roughly five miles west of the U.S. Airways Center (a.k.a. "the Snake Pit" or "the Purple Palace"), home of the Phoenix Suns basketball team, who came to town in 1968. Arizona's other professional basketball team is the Phoenix Mercury, which is a member of the Women's National Basketball Association.

Invented Here

Among the Grand Canyon State's numerous sports is sled-dog racing, sometimes held in northern Arizona. But "dog racing" strictly means greyhound racing, which was invented in the state. The year was 1909 when an engineer named Owen P. Smith demonstrated his new invention, a "mechanical rabbit" in Tucson. His device transformed the ancient sport of coursing (two or more greyhounds released to chase down live game) into a modern sport. Speaking of ancient, the word "greyhound" does not come from the color but from the Celtic word for dog, *grech.* The thrill of the sport is the speed—greyhounds can reach 40.9 miles per hour, or almost as fast as the 45 miles per hour of a girl shot from a cannon.

American Karate Started in Arizona

Speaking of packing a punch, karate, from the Japanese *kara-te* ("empty hand") was invented by Gichin Funakoshi in 1936, and the first karate school in North America opened in 1946, in Phoenix. Robert Trias (1923–89) learned the martial art in Okinawa, began teaching it to some friends in his backyard in Phoenix, then opened that first school—whose first students included a lot of Arizona State Highway Patrol officers. Trias also founded the United States Karate Association, and today he is known as "the Father of Karate in America."

DID YOU KNOW?

Allen Pitts, who was inducted into the Canadian Football Hall of Fame in 2006, was born in Tucson, Arizona. A receiver for the Calgary Stampeders, he set so many records (including 117 career touchdowns) that when he retired in 2000, his jersey number, 18, was also retired.

Not From Here, But Here Anyway

Other sports, while not invented in Arizona, thrive here. Football: Arizona's NFL team is the Arizona Cardinals, and our Arena Football League is the Arizona Rattlers. We also have a professional lacrosse team, the Arizona Sting and *three* pro ice-hockey teams. Wayne Gretzky moved to Arizona to coach (and co-own) the Phoenix Coyotes, a NHL team. Arizona's other two pro ice hockey teams are the Phoenix Roadrunners, which belongs to the East Coast Hockey League, and (in Prescott Valley) the Arizona Sundogs, which is in the Central Hockey League. Arizona also has a professional softball team, the Arizona Heat, in the National Pro Fastpitch League—the only professional women's softball league in the United States.

Baseball

Arizona today is above all a baseball state. Now the spring training home of the Chicago Cubs, the City of Mesa has been the state's major baseball destination for more than half a century. But 10 other clubs also come to Arizona for spring training in the "Cactus League." The Chicago White Sox and the Colorado Rockies train in Tucson. Along with the Chicago Cubs in Metro Phoenix (Phoenix, Glendale, Surprise, Scottsdale and Tempe): the Milwaukee Brewers, the Los Angeles Angels of Anaheim, the Los Angeles Dodgers, the Oakland Athletics, the San Diego Padres, the San Francisco Giants, the Kansas City Royals, the Seattle Mariners, the Texas Rangers and the Cleveland Indians. Residents and tourists spend $110 million per year to see Cactus League spring baseball games in Arizona.

Established in 1998, the Arizona Diamondbacks, winner of the 2001 World Series, train in Tucson and play out of their home stadium, Chase Field, in Phoenix. The Tucson Sidewinders, a minor league team established in 1969, moved to Reno, Nevada, in 2008.

There is also baseball here in the fall. The Arizona Fall League, owned and operated by all 30 Major League Baseball (MLB) clubs, is considered the first entry into the major leagues. Each August, MLB holds a draft to determine who will be sent to the Arizona Fall League teams.

DID YOU  **KNOW?**

Phoenix resident Linda Cobb is the great-granddaughter of baseball legend Ty Cobb. She herself is also nationally famous as the "Queen of Clean," having appeared on *Oprah* as a cleanliness counselor and home-cleaning authority.

Motor Racing

The only American cities with records of hosting Indy-style racing events longer than Phoenix's are Indianapolis and Milwaukee. Phoenix International Raceway (PIR) located west of Phoenix in Avondale, is a one-mile track with room for 76,800 fans. In comparison, Tempe's Sun Devil Stadium, site of Super Bowl XXX, seats only 76,000 fans. Race fans at PIR thrill every year to these NASCAR events: the Phoenix 150 (Craftsman Truck Series), the Arizona Travel 200 (Nationwide Series), the Bashas' Supermarkets 200 (Nationwide Series), the Checker Auto Parts 500 (Sprint Cup Series) and the Subway Fresh Fit 500 (Sprint Cup Series). Meanwhile, in Chandler, Firebird International Raceway has both drag races and speedboat races—as well as monster truck shows.

Gentlemen—and Lady: Start Your Engines!

In 2005, Scottsdale resident Danica Patrick, a cheerleader turned professional racecar driver, became the fourth woman ever to qualify for the Indianapolis 500.

Speaking of Cars and Trucks…
The City of Goodyear (Maricopa County) was named for the
Goodyear Tire and Rubber Company. The nearby City of
Litchfield Park was named for Paul W. Litchfield, a Goodyear
Rubber Co., executive.

Fore!

"Fore!" is the short form of the early British golfer's warning,
"Look out before!" There are 338 golf courses in Arizona.
Golfers here played 11,643,987 rounds of golf (18 holes) in
2004. Sixty-eight percent of the people who play golf in the
state are Arizonans, 29 percent are from other states and three
percent are visitors from other countries. The overall economic
impact of the golf course industry on Arizona is roughly
$3.5 billion per year and supports 17,000 jobs. Golf facilities
spend approximately $2.5 million for pesticides, $3.0 million for
herbicides, $8.0 million for fertilizer and $27.3 million for irrigation water, every year. Some people complain about golf
courses "wasting" water in the desert, but golf courses account
for only two percent of the state's water consumption. In 2004,
Arizona golf facilities occupied a total of 44,454 acres.

DID YOU KNOW?

Comedian Bob Hope played in every Phoenix Open from 1939 to 1991—52 years!

The Other Redcoats
Two years after the creation of Maricopa County in 1871, the Royal Montreal Golf Club became the first golf club in North America. Players were required to wear red coats, white flannel trousers and white gloves.

And They're Off!

Arizona has two major horseracing tracks, one in Prescott Valley and one in Phoenix. Both are one-mile tracks and host both thoroughbred and quarter horse races. Opened in Phoenix on January 7, 1956, Turf Paradise has one of the longest seasons of thoroughbred racing in the country. One of the main events there each February is the Turf Paradise Derby, an official prep race for the Kentucky Derby. Prescott Downs, in Prescott, opened in 1959, closed in 2000, and then reopened in nearby Prescott Valley as Yavapai Downs, which could almost be called Mile-High Downs—it's at an elevation of 5000 feet.

DID YOU  KNOW?

America's most highly decorated soldier in World War II, Audie Murphy, loved both horseracing and Arizona—at his ranch near Tucson he bred both quarter horses and thoroughbreds.

Skidding!

Skid was the Old Norse word for a snow ski—the last thing one might expect to find in Arizona. But the state most famous for its heat is only slightly less famous for its ski slopes. In Southern Arizona: Mount Lemmon Ski Valley, 9157 feet atop the Catalina Mountains, up to 16 feet of snow each year. At the base of the Catalinas is the city of Tucson. In Eastern Arizona: Williams Ski Area, in Williams, 7500–8100 feet; and in the White Mountains, Sunrise Park Resort, 9200–11,000 feet. Owned and operated by the White Mountain Apache Tribe, Sunrise, with 800 acres of skiing and snowboarding on three interconnected mountains, is Arizona's largest ski resort, and it gets up to 29 feet of snow each winter. In Northern Arizona: Arizona Snowbowl & Flagstaff Nordic Center, 14 miles north of Flagstaff, with a base elevation of 9300 feet and a chairlift to 11,500 feet. Opened in 1938, the Snowbowl is one of the oldest ski areas in the country. Also north of Flagstaff is the Wing Mountain Recreation Area, and just south of Flagstaff is the Mormon Lake Ski Tour Center.

DID YOU  KNOW?

In Summerhaven, a small community near the ski slopes atop Mt. Lemon, just north of Tucson, one of the original 39 Disney Mouseketeers bought the Alpine Lodge: Don Underhill.

Boxing Greats

Born in Winkelman in 1962, Louie Espinoza was Arizona's first world champion boxer. In 1987 he became the World Boxing Association Super Bantamweight Champion, and two years later the World Boxing Organization Featherweight Champion. He had a career record of 52 wins (44 by knockout) and 12 losses (one by knockout).

Born in Phoenix in 1967, Michael Carbajal, a four-time world champion boxer, was nicknamed "Little Hands of Stone." With a career record of 49 wins against four losses, with 33 wins by knockout, Carbajal was elected to the International Boxing Hall of Fame in 2006.

AMAZING ARIZONA Arizona is the Wal-Mart of states for outdoors activities. Under one "roof," we have pretty much everything: hiking, rock-climbing, spelunking, tubing (floating down a river on an inner tube), camping, birding, horseback riding, hunting, bow hunting, bow fishing (archery for fish), night "hunting" (driving on rural roads at night to catch glimpses of Arizona's nocturnal creatures from rattlesnakes to mountain lions), falconry, fishing…whatever the outdoor activity, it can be found here.

Some Fishing Feats

Species	Record	Where/When
Apache trout	5 lb. 15.50 oz.	Hurricane Lake, 1993 (world record)
Arctic grayling	1 lb. 9.76 oz.	Lee Valley Lake, 1995
Bluegill	3 lb. 15.68 oz.	Goldwater Lake, 2004
Brook trout	4 lb. 15.20 oz.	Sunrise Lake, 1995
Brown trout	22 lb. 14.50 oz.	Reservation Lake, 1999

Species	Record	Where/When
Carp	37 lb. 0.00 oz.	Bartlett Lake, 1987
Cutthroat trout	6 lb. 5.00 oz.	Luna Lake, 1976
Desert sucker	2 lb. 10.75 oz.	Verde River, 1992
Flathead catfish	71 lb. 10.24 oz.	San Carlos Lake, 2003
Largemouth bass	16 lb. 7.68 oz.	Canyon Lake, 1997
Northern pike	32 lb. 5.60 oz.	Ashurst Lake, 2004
Rainbow trout	15 lb. 9.12 oz.	Willow Springs Lake, 2006
Smallmouth bass	7 lb. 0.96 oz.	Roosevelt Lake, 1988
Striped mullet	5 lb. 2.24 oz.	Fortuna Pond, 2004
Tilapia	7 lb. 8.80 oz.	Saguaro Lake, 2002
Walleye	16 lb. 1.76 oz.	Show Low Lake, 2002

Outdoors is Big Business

Being outdoors is great fun for the individual, and great news for the state. Every year in Arizona, 255,000 anglers spend $831.5 million on equipment and trip-related expenditures, and 135,000 hunters account for an additional $126.5 million in retail sales. This combined $958 million in spending creates an economic impact of $1.34 billion to the state, supports more than 17,000 jobs, provides residents with $314 million in salary and wages and generates more than $58 million in state tax revenue.

"Non-consumptive wildlife-related recreations" (an Arizona Game and Fish designation), especially birding and hiking, have an even bigger economic impact on Arizona every year: $1.5 billion. In addition, "watchable wildlife recreation" supports over 15,000 jobs in the state, providing a total household income of $430 million and generating more than $57 million in state taxes.

RECIPES FOR SMILES

Saying "Hello" in Arizona

In Spanish: *¡Hola!*

In Apache: *Da go Te'*

In Jicarilla Apache: *Dáazho*

In Navajo: *Yá'át'ééh*

Seven Steps to 12 Terrific Arizona Tortillas

1. Gather the ingredients:

   2 cups all-purpose flour

   ¼ cup vegetable shortening

   ½ tsp. salt

   ½ tsp. baking powder

   ¾ cup warm water

2. In a bowl, mix the flour, salt, baking powder and vegetable shortening until the mixture resembles fine meal.

3. Add the warm water, a little at a time, working the mixture into a big dough ball.

4. On a floured surface, knead until the dough is smooth and elastic.

5. Divide dough into 12 smaller balls, then cover and let stand for at least 30 minutes.

6. On a floured surface, roll each ball into a six-inch diameter tortilla.

7. Place each tortilla on a pre-heated griddle or cast iron skillet and cook till medium golden on both sides.

10 GREAT REASONS TO LIVE IN ARIZONA

10. There's a Millionaires Club waiting for you to join up as soon as you qualify.

9. Arizona ranks in the top 10 of states that are "business friendly" in the U.S.

8. Arizona is the best state in the nation to see and appreciate cultural diversity.

7. The sun shines an average of 323 days a year here.

6. You can be snowbound in winter only if you want to be. (Otherwise, just live in central or southern Arizona.)

5. You get to drive on *real* Arizona highways instead of just look at the pictures in *Arizona Highways.*

4. You get to tell your out-of-state friends, "I live in the state with more rattlesnakes than anywhere else—but they rarely bite!"

3. If you get convicted, you get to wear pink underwear and eat green bologna in Sheriff Joe's world-famous Tent City.

2. No hurricanes, serious earthquakes, California-style mudslides or major floods, and no supertanker oil spills.

1. When California falls off, you'll have beachfront property.

ABOUT THE ILLUSTRATORS

Peter Tyler

Peter is a recent graduate of the Vancouver Film School's Visual Art and Design and Classical animation programs. Though his ultimate passion is in filmmaking, he is also intent on developing his draftsmanship and storytelling, with the aim of using those skills in future filmic misadventures.

Roger Garcia

Roger Garcia is a self-taught artist with some formal training who specializes in cartooning and illustration. He is an immigrant from El Salvador, and during the last few years, his work has been primarily cartoons and editorial illustrations in pen and ink. Recently he has started painting once more. Focusing on simplifying the human form, he uses a bright minimal palette and as few elements as possible. His work can be seen in newspapers, magazines, promo material and on www.rogergarcia.ca

Patrick Hénaff

Born in France, Patrick Hénaff is mostly self-taught. He is a versatile artist who has explored a variety of media under many different influences. He now uses primarily pen and ink to draw and then processes the images on computer. He is particularly interested in the narrative power of pictures and tries to use them as a way to tell stories.

ABOUT THE AUTHORS

Paul Soderberg

Paul Soderberg was born in Los Angeles, CA, and grew up in Asia. But it was only after attending college in Arizona, he knew he had found his home. A published novelist, Paul tried his hand as a taxi-driver, tomato-packer and Peace Corps volunteer in Afghanistan before finding a career as a writer. At 16, he was Guest Curator of Herpetology at The National Museum of Thailand and is currently a collector of six of the world's seven known specimens of *Isopeltys glyndelstoppei*—a legless lizard.

ABOUT THE AUTHORS

Lisa Wojna

Lisa is the co-author of more than a dozen trivia books, as well as being the sole author of nine other non-fiction books. She has worked in the community newspaper industry as a writer and journalist and has traveled all over the world. Although writing and photography have been a central part of her life for as long as she can remember, it's the people behind every story that are her motivation and give her the most fulfilment.

BLUE
BIKE
BOOKS

More madcap trivia from Blue Bike Books...

CAT TRIVIA
Humorous, Heartwarming, Weird & Amazing
Diana MacLeod

The most popular pet in North America is mysterious yet companionable, ferocious but cuddly, wild and domestic. Cats fascinate us with their exotic yet familiar ways. For cat lovers, this is a must-have.

Softcover • 5.25" x 8.25" • 224 pages
ISBN10: 1-897278-26-8 • ISBN13: 978-1-897278-26-0 • $14.95

DOG TRIVIA
Humorous, Heartwarming & Amazing
Wendy Pirk

Humans have lived alongside dogs for millennia, but there's more to them than just tail wags, a love for car rides and chasing tennis balls. It is not surprising that there are so many weird facts and fascinating tales about "man's best friend."

Softcover • 5.25" x 8.25" • 208 pages
ISBN10: 1-897278-36-5 • ISBN13: 978-1-897278-36-9 • $14.95

GROSS AND DISGUSTING THINGS ABOUT THE HUMAN BODY
Joanna Emery

The human body may be a wonder of natural engineering, but it can also be pretty gross and bad-smelling. In this fearless little book, find the answers to such profound questions as why are boogers green, why do farts smell and where does belly button lint come from?

Softcover • 5.25" x 8.25" • 224 pages
ISBN10: 1-897278-25-X • ISBN13: 978-1-897278-26-0 • $14.95

Available from your local bookseller or by contacting the distributor,
Lone Pine Publishing • 1-800-518-3541

www.lonepinepublishing.com